Tackling the
Poverty of Nations

Tackling the Poverty of Nations

Why So Many Are Poor and What We Can Do About It

George R. Grant

Library of Congress Control Number: 2008903329
ISBN: Hardcover   978-1-4363-3583-6
                 Softcover   978-1-4363-3582-9

This book was printed in the United States of America.

Caveat

This publication is an expression of the author's views. It is sold with the understanding that neither the publisher nor the author is engaged in rendering legal, accounting, or investment advice. If such advice or other expert assistance is required, the services of a professional should be sought.

To order additional copies of this book, contact:
Xlibris Corporation
1-888-795-4274
www.Xlibris.com
Orders@Xlibris.com
40427

CONTENTS

ACKNOWLEDGMENTS

More than fifty years of work should require many thank-yous, but I am afraid I have forgotten almost all who have helped. Therefore I will mention only those who have made this book possible in the past year or so. I'll start with my wife, Bernice, who has stood by me, helped and supported me for many years, and kept me going recently despite my frail health. Then I will mention a few who have helped me in extraordinary ways, such as Gillian Watts, my editor and rewriter, who organized and tidied the whole book, corrected details, clarified the theses, and in general made a clear manuscript out of a series of disjointed essays—many thanks! I thank the principal friends who have encouraged and corrected me in my analysis: Peter Carstens, my first reader, who put me in touch with Gillian Watts; Alan Cairns, who early on helped to put my pieces of arguments into one general thesis; Cliff Jutlah, who, as a friend of long standing from a similar background, many times discussed the themes with me; Vangel Vesovski, who challenged and taught me truths from an Austrian School background; and

Donna Ebers, who skilfully laid out and typed the manuscript repeatedly, putting herself out to do so when asked.

After these exceptional people come several more out-of-the-ordinary friends who have helped in several ways (in alphabetical order): John R. Ing, gold and currency expert; Judge Julius Isaac, leader of men; Denise Jacobs, close friend; John Jaffray, close friend and investment adviser; Stewart Jamieson, neighbouring farmer and helper; Bruce Lewis, self-sufficient environmentalist and handyman; Doug and Daphne Overhill, close friends and skilled and critical conversationalists; Armando Perez, humanist right-wing critic; Bruce Roberts, close friend, community leader, businessman, farmer, adviser, and environmentalist; Linda Schofield, close friend and left-wing adviser; Steve Sperling, large-scale landlord and source of worldly wisdom; Andrew Turvey, my source of government statistics; Jack Wallace, close friend and discussion partner; Clare White, close friend and source of ideas; and Ian Woods, close friend and strong left-wing critic.

As usual, all weaknesses, errors, and omissions are mine.

Importantly, in addition, I would like to add Hazel Que, Jason Paul, Ashley Nuico, Jaclyn d' Auria and Sherwin Soy of Xlibris for more-than-contractual help with publishing this book.

FOREWORD

This book is the culmination of serious thought given by George Grant to the question of how to alleviate the problem of poverty in many parts of the world. I first met him as a graduate student in economics at the University of Toronto in the late sixties, and I admire him for his tenacity of purpose. For him the issue is less one of wealth creation than one of satisfying basic human needs.

Part of the solution that Grant proposes is what he calls "reverse mercantilism." Under mercantilism, a poor nation (or a poor region within a country) received much of its income from domestically produced goods that merchants shipped to richer nations. The result was that the poor country, with its limited ability to expand exports, found itself in a trap of low consumption possibilities. Reverse mercantilism involves exportation of the abundant factor of production—labour services through migration—to richer countries, and patriation of income earned abroad by such workers back to the poor country. This could be a useful supplement to traditional forms of foreign aid.

Another part of Grant's solution is reform of the monetary system to strengthen the role of "commodity money." Over many decades countries have built their monetary bases on government debt and confidence in their ability to manage it. In Grant's view, this trend has created a foundation for worldwide inflation, which takes its toll most conspicuously in poor countries. He therefore proposes a shift in the monetary base from debt to real commodities such as precious metals. In principle, the resulting regime would be akin to the system that the world relied on for two and a half decades after the Second World War, a period of relatively low inflation.

I hope that this book will encourage those who share Grant's vision and provoke thought among those who are actively searching for solutions.

—Clifford Jutlah, PhD

PREFACE

Wherever you go, poverty surrounds you, though it is often conveniently out of sight. Also almost everywhere you go, there are people who would like to do something about it. But most do not know what to do, and much aid is wasted. Accordingly I set out to learn to do my part, and after half a century's study and experience, I think I have found some ways to advance the study of poverty alleviation. Now I am writing down some of what I have observed and learned, unfortunately leaving a lot behind, especially on environmentalism, which would have required another book. I hope this limited publication will prove helpful.

Without trying to write some of the book into this preface, I would like to say that it is based more on practical experience and observation, plus introspection, than on book study and theory. Theory is necessary to help one understand reality, but it should be based on real life. Therefore this book is written about what I have seen and done, where I have been, and what I have discovered; it is not loaded with references, but informed by reflection on and analysis of what I have experienced, aided by study. I think that this characteristic gives it greater value, even if less academic clout. I have tried to make it both realistic and interesting.

Please note that the wording of the title, *Tackling the Poverty of Nations*, does not place any limits on the causes of poverty or the location of those nations. But the text reveals that this book is not truly universal; it does not deal with all causes of poverty—such as war, refugees, displacement by natural causes, global warming, race, religion, hatred, history, etc.—nor with all locations, such as deserts or rainforests. But it does present a sample of the places to which I have been and the poverty problems there. Accordingly, it is scientific within those limits.

INTRODUCTION

What is this book about? Poverty—its major causes and its alleviation or removal. Why has it been written?

- Because the world isn't fair, and unfairness makes it hard to survive.
- Because people are suffering and aid isn't enough; they need more production and trade.
- Because few seem to understand the concepts that this book explains, and misunderstanding and poverty lead to conflict and war.
- Because the reality of poverty is so grave that I had to do something about it.
- Because I think this book could make a difference for the better. I have always wanted to help, and I think that I have found a realistic theoretical and practical approach that helps.

But in order to help, one must have a theory and some knowledge of the facts. And what better theory to start from than one based upon the facts? Many rural areas around the world are suffering poverty, due largely to such reasons as soil erosion and exhaustion, population explosions, drought and spreading deserts, expanding cities, deforestation, inflation, depression, etc. To survive this poverty, huge rural-urban and international migrations are taking place, taxing the resources of the receiving cities and leading to urban overcrowding, unemployment, and poverty.

To help tackle these resulting urban poverty problems, employment expansion is needed, but this expansion is hindered by a monetary system based on unbacked currency that threatens inflation along with expansion. Therefore, not only do we need rural development to reduce the influx into the cities, we need monetary reform to reduce urban unemployment without causing inflation, after which we will hopefully gain enough revenue to aid in rural development and alleviate the urban crush. This four-part theory is the essential thesis of this book, and its elements are reverse mercantilism, parallel gold-backed commodity money, urban-aided agricultural, rural, and regional development (along with appropriately adapted ideologies and constructive environmentalism).

In 1776 Adam Smith supplied us with an initial activating theory: "The great affair, we always find, is to get money."[1] Practically all of us strive, at great cost, to get money and/or the means of earning money. In a mercantilist society we fight to get these things and we don't willingly give them away to the poor—except when we don't lose by giving (as in teaching or medical aid)—and we certainly don't give if it enables the poor to compete with us. Consequently the poor are always with us. They seek development by generating exports to get money to buy what they want, including productive equipment. "Trade, not aid" is a frequent cry, especially when poorer nations realize that development and poverty alleviation come from export promotion and import substitution, not from imported aid.

This book uses practical examples to prove its theoretical points and to derive guiding theories. Canada was established by the metropolitan centre in order to promote British exports, facilitate the import of raw materials, and gain an export surplus—money— on the deal. Later Canada prospered by exporting a surplus of raw materials, as it does today. At least one Canadian province, Ontario, has deliberately used export promotion and import substitution to bring in surplus money and promote growth. The Ontario county of Simcoe has grown from self-sufficiency to hard-earned wealth entirely by export promotion and import substitution. My L0L1P0 small-farm experiment, located in Simcoe County, grew almost entirely by production expansion and export promotion. All of these projects succeeded through mercantilism, not through Keynesian monetary expansionism.

The L0L1P0 (pronounced "lollypo") small-farm experiment and some neighbouring farmers demonstrated the benefits of bringing outside money into a rural region and promoting regional development by developing production and export sales and generating wider benefits, which succeeded far better than equivalent aid dollars could have done. However, when production and export trade are less feasible, *reverse* mercantilism, or sending people out to bring money back instead of exporting goods to earn money, may have to be tried. The problem then switches to finding jobs under conditions of high urban unemployment.

But poverty can be caused not only by failures in production and trade—not bringing back enough surplus money to facilitate domestic commerce (the mercantilist argument)—but also by "market failure," or lack of circulation of money. This is known as inadequate demand, the central analytical core of the great world-shaking economic theories. It leads to two remedial tasks: to remedy the monetary system so as to get enough money demand without inflation (dealt with in chapters 1 and 2), and to remedy the money/income-distribution system so as to prevent inadequate demand, unemployment, and poverty (the task of chapter 3).

The mercantilist task of chapter 1 is aimed at exporting enough to prevent balance-of-payments deficits, devaluation, and inflation/loss of jobs. Chapter 2 approaches the task of remedying the monetary system, pointing out that our present bank money is created out of nothing and backed by nothing. If unemployment and poverty lead to inadequate monetary demand, printing more money leads quickly to inflation, lack of trust in money, and a need for restricting the monetary supply, leading back to inadequate demand, depression, and more poverty. The next step is to recommend a parallel, gold-backed "commodity money" to get around these monetary causes of poverty, by making scarce real money convertible into plentiful artificial money. This commodity money can be sold to the public with two guarantees—its gold content and the government's legal tender/convertibility contract printed on the coins—thus protecting the money unit and people's savings, discouraging inflation-accelerating speculative behaviour, reducing harmful inflation itself, and lessening the need for restrictive controls, thus reducing unemployment and poverty. The evils of the confidence game played by the banks with fraudulent "bank money" are spelled out in detail, showing it to be possibly the worst cause of suffering and poverty in the world's monetary economy.

Chapter 3, on ideologies, inequality and inadequate demand as causes of depression, poverty, and war, deals with what has become an important set of divisive ideas in the world economy, second only to religion, race, and land as causes for war. More attention is paid to the ideologies of mercantilism, capitalism, communism, socialism, Keynesianism, and monetarism—as causes of inequality, inadequate demand, recession/depression, inflation, unemployment, poverty, and war—than to all other analyses in the study of economics (except perhaps the studies of markets, trade, and finance to make money out of money in the richest cities of the world).

Chapter 4 completes this book's discussion of causes of and remedies for poverty by turning to the rural (and sometimes non-monetary) poverty caused more by production failure, price instability, overpopulation, desertification, ignorance, and so on than by mercantilism, ideologies, or monetary failure. The remedy discussed is agricultural, rural, and regional development. At the start of this process, rural poverty leads to rural-urban migration and reverse mercantilism (going away to earn money instead of exporting goods as a means of survival). The rural-urban influx leads to crowding in the poorer areas of cities, as well as to mass unemployment and urban poverty in the absence of the recommended parallel, gold-backed currency to stimulate growth without inflation. In the hopeful future, urban "real money" finance and educated expertise will produce urban prosperity and assist rural development and balanced growth, reducing both the rural destitution and urban poverty that have been aggravated by the rural-urban influx.

Chapter 5 discusses some other approaches to the problem of poverty and sums up this book in some detail, illustrating reverse mercantilism, the workings of parallel, gold-backed commodity money, the problems of ideological/inequality conflict, and some suggested mechanisms of agricultural and rural/regional development. It also discusses investment implications of the analysis and recent markets, as well as the practical details of working with a small farm.

An Autobiographical Note

I was born into comfortable circumstances in Trinidad in 1933, and in my early years lived and moved among relatively poor black people. After the Second World War I moved to South Africa, where the shockingly poor black people were kept "apart," except in such places as Adams Mission Station, where my father was principal. At Adams I looked out from our house (Emsebeni, or "at the top of the hill") and saw beyond the mission great stretches of ruined land and dilapidated huts. They contrasted sharply with the mansions and plantations of the wealthy whites, and I began to question why, and what could be done about such poverty next to such wealth.

I was moved by Alan Paton's great book *Cry, the Beloved Country*, especially his sentence "The soil cannot keep them any more" and his descriptions of the rural poverty of the Africans and their desperate migration to the slums of the white men's cities. That book persuaded me to start my odyssey—a quest to tackle poverty—by taking a degree in agriculture. But a near-fatal motorbike accident, plus my family's being forced to leave South Africa for opposing apartheid, put my plans on hold for a while. Later, after studying economic development at Oxford, I came to Canada, home of my father's family.

In Canada I worked in various government departments concerned with public welfare, economic development, foreign aid, tariffs for less developed countries, and agriculture. I began the L0L1P0 small-farm experiment to see if such an operation could provide some ideas to help alleviate the rural poverty that leads to rural-urban influx and poverty in city slums. One outcome of that experience was a small book, the first of several.

The L0L1P0 Experiment

My book based on the L0L1P0 experiment was *Trying to Help: Small Farmers and Large Economies*. I had not wanted to write about rural poverty and development without having first experienced a little of both myself, and I am glad I put myself through that experience. I also wanted to see how much could be done by small farms to alleviate rural poverty, and in what ways. So I bought and redeveloped a small farm myself, noting its potentials and its limits, particularly the hard labour and practical management needed and the marketing problems that had to be faced. I discovered that agricultural development was a job that required skills, experience, dedication, and outside help, credit, and learning—not a task that you could hand over to destitute people who would not be able to meet all these challenges without help and supervision. Accordingly, I drew up a scheme that would provide such supervision and assistance to landless people: a system of leased small farms, split off from larger government-purchased farms, to which the new farmers would be given title as a source of supervised credit. This system has the potential for "spread effects" of these new investments, jobs, and products in the rural areas (such as rural repopulation and reduced rural-urban migration), plus increased incomes and prosperity in place of poverty.

In addition to these theoretical purposes and plans, I had to operate practically to develop my own small farm from scratch. The land was bare—all but the maple trees had been cleared, so I planted a thousand more—and was furnished with a house, a couple of old barns, and electricity. There was practically nothing else of use except an access road, two acres of good soil, one acre of rough grass, and one acre of house, trees, and lawn. It was both fortunate and significant that my wife had a job as a teacher!

We moved in and I started spending my remaining capital on fencing, a well, egg-producing chicken facilities, goats for milking, a tractor, a rototiller and other farm and gardening equipment, chickens and feed, seeds and fertilizer, etc. I only just managed, thanks to sixteen-hour days and help from family I would not have been able to manage without my wife's capable "non farm" work: salary, housework, children, etc., and the children kicking in when needed and neighbours, until my existing gardening skills and newly learned egg-farming skills produced bumper yields on a small scale: about $30,000 gross revenue per year. That would now have been many inflationary times more. It wasn't all that long before I couldn't take it any more and "retired" to a desk job in government that brought in much more money for far less work, (a revelation in itself).

But I had proved that a well-equipped-and-managed small farm could produce a living income on a small scale, one much better than that of unemployed city dwellers, at least. Small farmers who work hard and with skill and are supported by credit and good advice can become prosperous, make wise land reform programs work, and help promote agricultural, rural, and regional development, thus reducing rural poverty, rural-urban migration, and urban overcrowding and poverty. It is possible, although it is slow, demanding work—not a task that can be carried out by ideologies and plans and unskilled labour alone.

As my experiment confirmed, without help such a project as the L0L1P0 small farm is beyond the capabilities and resources of landless settlers. But it shows what can be done on a few acres if outside resources are available and used productively, for example on a government- or university-operated agricultural development and teaching station. Small homesteads can be purchased on credit, and with infrastructures and guidance can be developed to produce for their own use, debt repayment, and export sales. The spread effect would stimulate local community and wider regional development, helping to alleviate both rural and urban poverty.

Trying to Help described how I developed my small farm from scratch into a viable enterprise, helping me to better understand what I was studying. By writing about my experience I hoped to help those who wanted to promote rural development through producing goods for sale and for export. It was an attempt to make practical my ideas about reducing poverty by doing it myself. The L0L1P0 example has been followed by local farmers, and its text material and diagrams have been copied: I hope its lessons can be applied more widely. In chapter 1 of this book I describe the L0L1P0 experiment further and discuss its implications for the relief of poverty.

Earlier Approaches

Before *Trying to Help*, I had written two other small books: *Canadian Rural Development Lessons for South African and Other Third World Rural Regions* and *Canada Savings Coins: A Proposal to Help Remove the Monetary Causes of the Poverty of Nations*. The first, based on general reading about economic development and grounded in my own small-farm experiment, advanced ideas aimed at increasing rural income. Its goal was to check the desperate migration of the rural poor to city slums, thus relieving both rural poverty and depopulation and urban poverty and overpopulation, through a poverty-relief program that could be adopted on a large scale. The book also tackles the conundrum that, beyond certain limits, intensification of agricultural output and farm and rural self-sufficiency are impossible. Both complete self-sufficiency and support of growing populations require balanced and diversified rural/regional development, funds from reverse mercantilism, and rural village growth-points. Reverse mercantilist sources of "outside" money—to stimulate rural farm and village development—and parallel commodity money—to help expand urban economies—can develop both types of region at the same time, reducing rural poverty and out-migration while giving urban development a chance to catch up with growing needs.

Canada Savings Coins is a proposal that introduces parallel commodity money into the discussion of poverty alleviation. Many countries today suffer from both high unemployment (that is, poverty) and fear of inflation. This (justified) fear of inflation impedes the use of stimulative money and fiscal policies to fight unemployment, because stimulative policies lead to either inflation, devaluation, more inflation, restrictive policies, and higher unemployment, or to more inflation and the threat of monetary and economic collapse (that is, much more poverty). Thus non-stimulative policies are often maintained and unemployment and poverty remain high, rendering Keynes irrelevant. However, if the government introduced an anti-inflationary gold-backed money unit—such as the book's Canada Savings Coins—to run parallel to the inflationary, unbacked bank-money unit, savings could be protected and inflation could be reduced and become less feared. This modification of the monetary institution and its units to help alleviate unemployment and poverty is part of the message of the present book.

Incentive and Justification: Poverty in Apartheid South Africa

Even more influential than my experiences of rural poverty, reading of Alan Paton and glimpses into urban poverty in South Africa and the West Indies was the report of the Second Carnegie Inquiry into Poverty in South Africa,[2] which brought home for me the heartrending tragedy of extreme poverty. However, while it provides encyclopedic documentation of "facts" and proximate "causes" of poverty, it offers little in the way of a clear thesis of fundamental causes that could be tackled other than by small provisions of aid. For example, poverty in the native reserves is said to be caused by things like soil erosion, but little is made of the ideology of apartheid, as expressed by Daniel Lindley in 1845: "Reserve for the Natives so little land that they will not be able to subsist on it, and will then have to ask permission to live on the lands of [the whites], which will be granted on condition that they labour for their landlords"[3]—a deliberate policy of creating poverty for millions.

Going even further back, the gold standard led nations to fight for gold, trade surpluses, and colonies through mercantilism, imperialism, colonialism, capitalism, and war. Under these banners, whites with guns conquered darker-skinned peoples and took their lands, pushing them onto minute pieces of poor-quality land or into virtual (and sometimes actual) slavery—and long-lasting poverty—actions that were justified by missionaries who gave them the Bible in exchange for their lands. In South Africa, when blacks could no longer survive on their patchwork moonscapes and began to migrate to the white cities, apartheid was introduced, under which whites kept the native Africans "apart" from whites' lands, society, government and other sources of wealth and power.

The amazing Nelson Mandela negotiated to get power from the whites. He was helped by reverse mercantilism, under which black migrant labourers swamped the whites in the cities, forcing a handover of power. However, he did not get the wealth and the land, the lack of which perpetuates black inequality and

Figure 1: South Africa—abandoned arable land scarred by gully erosion. (Source: D. Hobart Houghton and Edith M. Walton. *The Economy of a Native Reserve: Keiskammahoek Rural Survey.* Vol. 2. Pietermaritzburg: Shuter and Shooter, 1952.)

poverty today, aggravated by gently disguised mercantilism and confidence money. We can look to the Commission's report for further details.

In 1980 in South Africa as a whole, including the reserves, the proportion of the total population living below subsistence was estimated to be 50 percent. For those living in the reserves, no less than 81 percent were in dire poverty. Inequality was so great that South Africa's GINI coefficient (which measures disparity) was the highest of all the countries for which data were available. And the numbers of the landless, homeless, and totally destitute (that is, with an income of less than C$20 per month) have risen dramatically. South Africa is simultaneously the richest and poorest region in Africa.

Soil erosion is another major poverty-causing problem (see Figure 1). In combination with deteriorating vegetation— desertification—it is held by some to be far and away the most serious of the many problems facing Africa. When land is destroyed, those who have nowhere else to live have nothing to sustain them. They have to go as beggars to the cities, adding to the ranks of the unemployed poor, who have enough problems already. Excessive and improper use of the land creates deeper and deeper impoverishment for all those who have no land or job elsewhere. In addition, South Africa is on average too poor and the African population relatively too large for welfare to be enough—and there was no welfare when the report was written.

Figure 2: South Africa—fetching firewood. (Source: Houghton and Walton)

For people without money, fuel is hard to get. Millions of South Africans face enormous difficulties obtaining the fuel they need for cooking, warmth, and light in the absence of electricity (see Figure 2). The long-distance collecting of firewood has serious ecological consequences, such as deforestation, soil erosion, and desertification; similar results come from overcultivation and overgrazing. Water, especially clean drinking water, is scarce, precious, and sometimes expensive for the poor (see Figure 3). Drought can starve or kill entire populations. And rural blacks have nowhere else to go except the city slums, where half the inhabitants are unemployed. In addition, inadequate land and water lead to theft, poaching, and fighting over resources.

Figure 3: South Africa—going to fetch water. The people are so poor that they have no water in their homes, but have to trek long distances to carry back meagre supplies. Note the sheet erosion and desert-like conditions. (Source: Houghton and Walton)

Low wages are often the proximate cause of much poverty, and the wages earned by most Africans are below the poverty level. Lack of income leads to other problems such as malnutrition and other effects of extreme poverty. Old age pensions and remittances sent back home by migrants are critical to many rural dwellers, but they too are also routinely below the official poverty level. The broad pattern in the urban townships of South Africa can be described as a "universe of poverty"—and it is from these areas that the rescuing money is supposed to come. Unemployment among Africans is very high, with the report's estimates ranging from 20 to 50 percent (today they are 45-50 percent), and there is no unemployment insurance. (Attempts to provide welfare add to inflation problems).

The tragedies are indeed heartrending. Hunger and malnutrition plague a third to two-thirds of black and "coloured" children. Infant mortality and life-threatening diseases are rampant: gastroenteritis, cholera, typhoid, dysentery, measles, tuberculosis, and, of course, enough AIDS to cause population decline and societal breakdown in some regions. The overcrowding and inadequate housing conditions are overwhelming: shack dwellings with up to ten people per tiny room with no privacy, no electricity or running water, no sanitary facilities. There is little food and much drinking, especially in the massive compounds for male workers, which contain several thousand men in one space. Their families have been left behind and there is no way to send money home; noise pollution, violence, and crime are endemic. It is virtually impossible for blacks to get a good education.

The Commission report asks: What happens to the economy and the society of the areas from which the migrants have come? The answer is that the economy produces less but the people largely stay there and become poorer; society and the ecology collapse; disease, crime, and so on destroy both the rural and urban segments of the African population; poverty is perpetuated and worsens. All of these (plus the analyses in this book) combine to explain the proximate causes of poverty, but not the originating causes: mercantilism and dispossession; racism, discrimination, and disenfranchisement; monetary weaknesses causing additional mass unemployment and poverty; and gross inequalities in income and wealth, particularly in land ownership, that contribute to the devastating sickness of migrant labour. The report even concludes that the real question is the one that the commissioners specifically excluded—namely, how best to bring about political change that empowers the poor.

When I had read and absorbed the implications of this report, I wandered off to think what I had to do. The result is this book. (Many years later)

A Theory of Money, Poverty, and Inflation

Money and Poverty

Let us consider the economies of small places such as Simcoe County in Ontario, native reserves in South Africa, or small islands such as Grenada in the West Indies, which do not have the facilities to create their own convertible money. In such regions or nations, export revenues or convertible money income coming in from outside constitute the money supply—until these units leak abroad and drain away that money supply.[4]

A vital point to note is that, if outside income is spent immediately on imports of foreign goods (for example, at a trading post or chain store), no local income or economic stimulus results. Local economic (and perhaps social) life is dead and local poverty will be severe, with nothing to do, nothing to buy or invest with, and no ability to pay taxes to get community tasks done. It is then no wonder that such reserves and small economies are poor and depressed and hard to develop—there is little or no local money demand and the costs of producing and selling exports (except local produce) are beyond local means. But if half the outside income were spent on local goods and services, at each round of spending, local real money income would be equal to export income ($\frac{1}{2} + \frac{1}{2} \times \frac{1}{2} + \frac{1}{2} \times \frac{1}{2} \times \frac{1}{2} \ldots = 1$), and the local economy could come alive and grow.[5]

Now we can see where Adam Smith and the mercantilists came from and led to. In Adam Smith's day, when convertible gold money was scarce because banks had not yet won acceptance of their fraudulent bank money, there tended to be inadequate money (demand), depression, and poverty. Mercantilistic governments accordingly sought to bring in more money (gold) through a favourable balance of trade, that is, more exports than imports. The discipline of economics began principally as a means to achieve adequate demand in order to fight poverty.

Unfortunately, much capital was required for manufacturing and the export trade, and the profits earned tended to accumulate in the hands of capitalists who did not distribute them all to workers. So not all the money earned was spent, not all products could be sold, and inadequate demand and depressions followed, along with unemployment, poverty, and "immiserization of the proletariat." Marx blamed the capitalists, who he said paid the workers "less than the true value of their labour," rendering them unable to buy the products of their labour. He then called for revolution, expropriation, and capital to be placed in the hands of the state—again, to achieve adequate demand to fight poverty. This helped prepare the way for the socialists, who argued that expropriation was disruptive and not necessary. All that was needed, they claimed, was redistribution of income through taxes, higher wages and the introduction of a welfare state—again to seek adequate demand, with the addition of greater equality.

But world war and depression intervened, and a theoretical opening was created for Keynes and his disciples to oppose heavy taxes and to promise investment, full employment, adequate demand, and a welfare state through deficit spending—a policy that worked wonders for some decades, despite inflation (even runaway inflation) in many countries. Most recently, inflation and large-scale welfare, combined with the return of unemployment, has led to the rebirth of right-wing parties and governments and "monetarist" philosophers, who oppose high taxes, welfare, and inflation, introducing the danger of a return to inadequate demand and poverty.

We have thus seen more than a century of conflict over how to tackle inadequate demand, unemployment, and poverty. But in the midst of this big picture, the vital point has been largely missed that demand must be for *domestic* goods, and lasting poverty arises for those who cannot produce and export sufficient domestic goods *and* keep the return proceeds circulating in the domestic economy.

Money and Inflation

When nations suffered under inadequate demand that led to poverty and lack of production, they were only too glad to have banks create money to stimulate business, and the banks were happy to oblige. They created money that was not backed by gold and lent it out at interest to keen and trusting borrowers, who stimulated production, trade, and development with their skills, more workers and the new money. But along with borrowed money and expansion came inflation, bank failures, worthless money, monetary crises and collapses, periodically severe unemployment, depression, war, and mass poverty—again!

Eventually monetary authorities became hesitant about tackling poverty and its attendant woes through expansion of the money supply and low interest rates. They feared repeated crises and, particularly, more inflation (especially devaluation by foreigners). Therefore they did not always act strongly to use stimulative monetary and fiscal policies to fight recession, unemployment, and poverty because of the dangers of yet more inflation and the possible future need to revert to restrictive policies and even higher unemployment and poverty. Accordingly, even in conditions of high unemployment and poverty, non-stimulative policies have often been maintained for fear of the return of inflation.

But if the government were to introduce a gold-backed parallel commodity currency—anti-inflationary, capable of gradually increasing the money supply, and intrinsically valuable—with two values (a guaranteed minimum face value backed by the government, plus the value of its gold content), to run parallel with and convertible into the inflationary unbacked bank-money unit, we would have a long-sought-after real-value currency to protect our savings, reduce inflation, create employment, and generate profits for the government—thus fighting inflation, unemployment, and poverty at one stroke. The result of inaction would be accelerating, self-perpetuating inflation of the unbacked bank-money units, punctuated by crises, and we would never be able to reduce poverty.

Alternative Money Theory

As indicated at the beginning of chapter 4, we can sometimes see more clearly by looking down from above. When we do so, we can see people moving to and fro, earning and spending invisible promises or credits, or exchanging promises for goods and promises for promises (with numbers attached). These activities are part of a market system that regulates what is produced and consumed. These exchanges of promises or credits are recorded in an elaborate bookkeeping system, which keeps track of "ownership" of promises created out of nothing. These promises, created by exchanges out of nothing, are what people work for, live on and save, seldom questioning whether they will keep their promised value when their numbers rise from millions to billions to trillions and more.

These promises consist of nothing except stated claims on the national product which others accept and which are transferable: you can obtain products and services in exchange for them from others who have "confidence" that others will take them in turn, ad infinitum. (Inflation undermines that confidence.)

But if the whole of our monetary system depends on confidence or faith in a set of un-backed promises that can be destroyed by inflation, there is something desperately fragile about this system which should be reformed—by separating money into spending and saving components. If we do this, then, in the future, when the supply of money promises has expanded exponentially toward infinity, with infinitesimal value per unit, there will still be a distributed standard of value to integrate into our future distribution and value system.

This will not change our system dependent on an exchange of promises, some visible and some invisible, for goods and services and other promises. But the invisible money-credit-promises will remain created out of nothing except a promise (an IOU or a loan) to give you money in exchange for real assets, which promise (bank money) you obtain by believable or creditworthy promises to give back bank money plus interest or assets worth bank money plus interest. When this debt-promise cannot be fulfilled, the bank takes the asset backing, and it only loses when the asset backing, or security, becomes insufficient or illiquid. This has frequently been the case recently, even to the extent of threatening bank failures. If bank failures occur, bank deposits (money) would be wiped out, and the monetary economy would be brought down; so bank failures must be prevented—by injecting central bank—created money into the banking system, in an inflationary manner. This is what is happening now; so the next stage in our monetary saga is inflation, followed by rising interest rates and a monetary crash or by gradual inflation until everyone is poor.

CHAPTER 1

Tackling Poverty Through Trade and Migration: Mercantilism and Reverse Mercantilism

The Great Affair, we always find, is to get money;
when that is obtained, there is no difficulty in making
any subsequent purchase.
—Adam Smith, *The Wealth of Nations* (1776)

The Theories: Adam Smith and Today

Mercantilism is a theory about how to get rich by acquiring more money from exports to other nations than is spent on imports from other nations. Reverse mercantilism, accordingly, is a theory about how to escape poverty by learning from mercantilism. It is very simple: if some nations get rich by bringing in excess money, then other nations may be able to escape poverty by bringing in an excess of money (a trade surplus) from the rich nations and regions.

Writing in 1776, Adam Smith described the "mercantile system" theory about how our economy works: depression and poverty when there is inadequate money (demand), and prosperity when there is a favourable balance of trade, bringing in adequate money or demand:

> That wealth consists in money, or in gold and silver, is a popular notion which naturally arises from the double[1] function of money, as the instrument of commerce, and as the measure of value. In consequence of its being the instrument of commerce, when we have money we can more readily obtain whatever else we have occasion for, than by means of any other commodity.
>
> The great affair, we always find, is to get money; when that is obtained, there is no difficulty in making any subsequent purchase . . . . A rich country, then, in the same manner as a rich man, is supposed to be a country abounding in money; and to heap up gold and silver in any country is supposed to be the readiest way to enrich it.[2]
>
> In consequence of these popular notions, all the different nations of Europe, have studied every possible means of accumulating gold and silver in their respective countries . . . by watching over the balance of trade.[3]
>
> The two principles being established, however, that wealth consisted in gold and silver, and that those metals could be brought into a country which had no mines only

by the balance of trade, or by exporting to a greater value than it imported; it necessarily became the great object of political economy to diminish as much as possible the importation of foreign goods for home consumption, and to increase as much as possible the exportation of the produce of domestic industry. Its two great engines for enriching the country, therefore, were restraints upon importation, and encouragements to exportation . . . . The restraints upon importation . . . consisted sometimes in high duties [tariffs], and sometimes in absolute prohibitions [quotas, embargoes] . . . . Exportation was encouraged sometimes by drawbacks, sometimes by Bounties [subsidies], sometimes by advantageous treaties of commerce with foreign states, and sometimes by the establishment of colonies [e.g., Canada] in distant countries.[4]

In these words Adam Smith clearly describes the "commercial or mercantile system" as it was then and indeed is now, except for the replacement of gold and silver by bank money. Essentially the policy is to gain an advantage (a favourable balance of trade) by promoting exports and restricting imports in order to prevent foreigners getting an advantage—that is, more money, whereby we might lose money and income, purchasing power, and jobs via an unfavourable balance of trade. We seek to increase exports, for example, by subsidies to bring enough export money demand into domestic circulation, and to reduce imports and loss of money demand, for example, by restraints upon importation. In other words, we still think and justify our policy actions in mercantilist terms. Reverse mercantilism is mercantilism learned and applied by the victims of mercantilism, primarily in developing regions of the world: exports of labour, tourism and "invisible" services to bring surplus money (demand) back into the originating region.

In Canada, we ourselves have tariffs; we apply quotas (against poor countries' goods) and embargoes (against enemy countries' goods); we employ drawbacks (our GST "draws back" duties and excises on Canadian goods when they are exported); we enter into what we judge to be advantageous treaties of commerce (the Free Trade Agreement was believed to be advantageous because we expected to increase exports more than we would increase imports). We also keep tariffs higher for, apply more quotas to, and do not enter into trade agreements that we judge to be unfavourable with, poor or low-wage or unfriendly countries, as they do not seem to offer us equivalent export gains from freer trade. An exception was the General Preferential Tariff (GPT) program, under which we offered favourable tariff treatment to the poorest countries on goods that would not harm Canadian manufacturers (I worked for several years on that program). Our rich-nation international tariff system applies lower tariffs only to the Most Favoured (i.e., rich or friendly) Nations that will import as much more from us as we import from them under lower tariffs. We exclude the poor nations' goods, especially their higher-value-added manufactures, which would move money and demand, jobs, and profits to the poor nations. And we apply tariffs that rise with the degree of processing, so that we import raw materials and "add value" here to keep money and demand, jobs, and wealth at home, thus keeping the poor nations poor. Hence, mercantilism and protectionism are great causes of poverty.

Export Economies

Now we are primed to look at some evidence from Jonathan V. Levin's book *The Export Economies.*[5] Levin discusses the raw material export economies: those in which the principal activity in the monetary sector was the production of raw materials for export, leading to the development of an export economy.[6] Most of these economies, despite decades or even centuries of participation in international trade, have remained at low levels of economic development, with low levels of income (i.e., poverty) for most of their population but relatively high levels of income for the skilled people and capitalists from abroad. The latter immigrants sent a large part of their earnings—most of the export income—abroad to their home country and did not spend much locally except on imported luxuries. The resulting lack of domestic spending explains much of the lack of development in many export economies: no mass money market to stimulate industry, or inadequate demand. Instability of export volumes and prices abroad added to this weakness. All the resulting inequality, poverty, and lack of development for the locals has led to revolts in underdeveloped export economies, and not always successfully: in some cases the benefits went mainly to local elites, graft, and corruption while the greater part of the country remained beset by mass poverty and occasional revolutions. It is only in a few cases that the benefits of exports have spread to the wider population.

Mercantilism: Riches and Poverty

Mercantilism posits the benefits of a favourable balance of trade. If there were limited foreign trade and no domestic creation of money, and a region or nation was poor, with little money or income around, prices would be low and local sales would be sluggish—as in Simcoe County some decades ago. But when foreign sales increase and almost everyone is earning a higher income, local sales and prices rise, land prices also soar, and prosperity tends to reduce poverty. The results, as in Simcoe County, support the mercantilist argument about the benefits of a favourable balance of trade.

If we were to put this mercantile argument into Keynesian terms, we might say that leakage of money or expenditure into imports and out of the economy has to be offset—or, rather, more than offset—by an injection into the economy of new money or buying power from exports (or from deficit spending). This is necessary in order to stimulate the economy; to raise the equilibrium level of income and employment; to keep business buoyant, prosperous, and growing; and to reduce poverty.

The mercantilist argument was believed and acted upon long before Marx made his prediction that capitalist inequality would lead to inadequate demand, depression, imperialism, and war (and poverty). Mercantilist nations had repeatedly gone to war for imperialist reasons—to capture markets for manufacturers; sources of cheap raw materials, land, and fresh water; colonies and empires; and favourable trade balances—and capitalist, imperialist, and warlike nations have done so ever since. Today, however, some nations claim not to be mercantilist, or at least not militarily so, though they all seek to "capture" markets, own or protect resources (such as oil) on which they depend, "exploit" hinterlands, and so on. Every nation seeks to sell exports and to resist imports, and thus, by selfish, mercantilistic behaviour, to create poverty everywhere else.

Indeed, the mercantilist/imperialist tendency is almost universal, especially under conditions of crowding and scarcity. Competitive individuals, families, clans, tribes, ethnic groups, companies, and nations all try to acquire as many resources and/or sales as possible in order to provide adequate livelihoods, prestige and power, and so on—by conquest, purchase, hard work, and/or study, and by "saving" or resisting imports and purchases of foreign goods. In contrast, the poor are those who, persuaded by salesmen, bankers, and/or armies, have lost their money, land, properties, and independent livelihoods, or, instead of working hard, studying, and saving, have borrowed to spend and so have come into debt or become dispossessed. It seems that one must be either mercantilistic or poor! *Dispossessed* is indeed a useful descriptive/causative word for poverty.

Most approaches to the poverty problem fail partly because they do not understand or try to remedy the basic competitive, mercantilist, imperialist, dispossession causes of poverty. We compete in order to sell for money, not to serve, and we therefore compete with the poor. Then we hand out alms to those who fail—or who fail to understand and use mercantilist principles. So if, as Adam Smith says, "the great affair . . . is to get money," we strive, as our parents, competitors, markets, and society have urged us, to get the means—education, qualifications, reputation, money, land, capital—of getting money. These means cost a great deal and are a measure of power and prestige. And we don't give them away, except through education and some medical help, which don't cause us financial loss.

We also compete to acquire the means of getting money. We fight to get the land and the markets and never give them up, offering in return only a little replaceable income or consumer goods. You can't really help the poor unless you provide productive land, resources, capital, training, jobs, and markets for their products (including "reverse mercantilist" migrant labour) and/or the capital and skills to produce saleable products. But those assets are what everyone wants, and there is a great reluctance to give them away. This requirement is the essential problem of development: most people talk around it, but no one wants to give up their resources.

Foreign aid, for example, consists of *imports* to the recipients that compete with their domestic products. There is little discussion of assisting poor countries with their *exports*, the mercantilist remedy for poverty. (When I worked in Ottawa on import tariffs, I had to make sure that Canada received the benefit.) You don't help people to take away your own wealth, but you can help them to produce what you need. We cannot produce enough for the half of the world that is poor, yet we try to prevent the poor from producing what they need (or could sell to us without harm)—through our gift-aid, our hogging of resources, and our exclusion of products that might harm our own jobs and income.

Some "remedies" are, moreover, systematically harmful, even dangerous. For example, Marxists have told poor peoples that they can seize wealth and become rich. Keynesians have told them that they can create money and buying power and become rich. The rulers of newly independent countries have told them that they can push out the plantation economy and the foreign capitalists and become rich. And the rich nations (and their people) have said that the poor must do nothing to touch their property and wealth, because to do so would be terrorist and revolutionary and would destroy business confidence, leading to capital flight, currency and economic collapse, and even worse poverty (so it would, and does). None of these approaches works to remedy poverty and injustice. About the only examples of poor and colonial peoples becoming rich are those nations that have been able to become successful reverse mercantilists or surplus exporters and to sell (produce what others need and will take) more than they buy in the world markets. Having brought in outside money and stimulated their economies, they then distribute or diversify the wealth, finally increasing their output, or productivity, by investment in human and material capital—hopefully without destroying their environment. This is the mercantilist (or "staple export") formula, which also makes "Smithian" sense, as described earlier.

Rich countries, meanwhile, by means of mercantilist policies (and perhaps also armies, the media, and/or entrepreneurial capitalists), have been able to acquire export or resource sales stimuli, distribute and diversify these incoming stimuli widely to benefit their own nationals and increase domestic demand, and increase productivity through investments (and sometimes through violence and war). Poor countries, in contrast, have failed to acquire enough resources, surplus exports, distributed monetary stimuli, or increased output and productivity. The above mercantilist factors are probably the most important causes (other than money capital, as noted below) of prosperity and poverty, but they are not readily admitted to by Western economists, policymakers, and aid agency workers, and simply not "seen" by bookish economists. As a result, reverse mercantilist lessons and the above, cooperative instead of competitive trade practices are not taught or applied, and poor countries (other than "export economies") remain stricken with poverty.

Poor nations and poor peoples are thus the dispossessed, or those who never had anything. They are the military, competitive, and colonial (mercantile) failures and their descendants, kept poor by trade and personal failure and discrimination. They are not only sad cases of suffering and hardship and economically depressing and otherwise potentially dangerous problems, but also problems that are self-perpetuating and enforced from the outside as long as they survive. The rich nations and the favoured groups within nations try to keep it that way. They don't necessarily or explicitly intend to keep people poor; after all, they send out aid, volunteer workers, and medical and emergency help—consumption but not production goods; "good things" but not export or trade opportunities (they don't want to lose resources, jobs, or sales)—but they nevertheless do keep nations poor as they drive to acquire resources and gain markets. After capturing it by war or purchase, who would hand over an oil well or a sugar-refining industry,[7] with its jobs, trade benefits, and spin-offs, to a poorer nation or group of people? Although now becoming overshadowed by created-money capital "investments," gaining or holding on to productive capital, resources, and markets is the commercial or mercantilist road to riches (and, conversely, poverty).[8] Mercantilism is thus one of the prime causes of poverty.

Mercantilism and Canada

Canada, a rich nation dependent on resource exports, was established as a colony to increase markets for the home country's goods and to supply cheap raw materials in return. The Native peoples were dispossessed and remain poor to this day; they are still trying to claim back lost lands and are discriminated against when they try to export their labour to the cities. When they get angry about refusals to honour land treaties, the police and the army are called out against them. Some get shot and even killed, but justice is not done even then. Meanwhile Natives continue to die because of poverty, and our monetarily rich nation refuses to do anything about it.

Colonial Canada continued to develop around staple exports,[9] both expanding those exports and multiplying dependent, import-replacing industries and services, including government, within the scope of the export revenues. Later on, as the domestic market grew larger, Canada began to restrict imports, trying to take in only raw materials from poor countries for processing locally, and placing manufactures from rich countries behind tariffs while selling its own raw materials (and, later, finished goods) around the world to achieve a trade surplus, in true mercantilist fashion.

Gradually Canada developed and prospered because it exported more than it imported, distributed and diversified the proceeds, and increased output and productivity. This process was aided by foreign investment, which brought an additional inflow of money, skills, technology, capital, and entrepreneurs. Metropolitan investors and trading partners also gained, both because Canada was an economic colony that mostly exported cheap raw materials and imported more costly manufactured goods, and because it was a profitable source of wealth, returning to the metropolis plentiful "invisible" revenues (interest, dividends, capital gains, etc.). These revenue outflows, added to other import leakages from Canada, eventually became so large that they became a threat to the Canadian economy, a threat that expanded exports have thus far staved off.

In economic terms it can be said that Canada's whole economic history has been a mercantilist story. First, the mother country used

Canada as a source of raw materials and a market for manufactures, leaving very little hard currency behind (Canadians had to make do with barter, wampum, and beaver pelts). Then gradually Canada expanded its raw material export surpluses so greatly that its dollar became a hard currency and its trade surpluses made it into a rich nation. The country succeeded by reverse ("turnaround") mercantilism, turning around and exporting its way to prosperity, distributing the proceeds, and diversifying around the export base. Then economic development investments increased its output—productivity and exports—and staved off threats such as deficits on external payments and competition from low-priced goods from developing countries, by using more resource exports.

There is a kicker in this picture: Canada's oil and gas resource industries are so powerful, productive, and profitable that they are pushing up wage and other costs to a level that other Canadian industries can barely afford. There is thus pressure on both employment and prices. This is a non-mercantile distribution problem that I will not go into deeply here, except to say that Canadians should study the problems, policy responses, and results for other countries, such as Trinidad and Tobago, that face a similar situation (see, for example, Appendix A: The "Dutch Disease" Problem).

I can suggest that two major problems arise from such strong and profitable resource export industries: regionally much higher wage levels and a dollar that rises to uncompetitive levels. Solutions are difficult, but they probably should include more steeply progressive income taxes, restrictions on growth of the oil and gas industry, expanded pipelines to eastern Canada, and higher taxes on carbon fuels. None of these is likely to come about, although policies to increase productive investments outside of oil and gas (even "heritage funds") might be more acceptable. It was reported recently that Canada and Ontario have lost large numbers of manufacturing jobs in the past two to four years, and even the *Globe and Mail*'s *Report on Business* has said: "We are a resource rich nation and we should be creating valuable products from our natural resources, instead of shipping them raw to be manufactured elsewhere."[10] This is pure mercantilism, and some of the implications for Canada are indicated below.

In the Canadian economy, about 40 percent of the national income is earned through exports; something like 10 percent is earned by all industries competing in the home market with imports. These internationally competitive sectors in a sense support the whole economy (with international "convertible" money), including the 50 percent of the economy that is dependent on Canada's export earnings. Perhaps 10 percent is earned in private sectors—such as law, construction, retail, transportation, finance and medicine—that, while competing domestically, do not compete directly with imports that could take money or purchasing power abroad. And about 40 percent is taxed by and received from governments at all levels: health, about 10 percent; education, about 7 percent; unemployment insurance, pensions, welfare and other social benefits, perhaps around 15 percent. Administration, policing, defence, and so on account for the rest.

The exact percentages do not matter here because they do not alter the general point that about 50 percent of the Canadian labour force does not work for internationally competitive industries, and many do not work under competitive industry conditions at all. This 50 percent is protected from direct vulnerability to foreign low wages, devaluation, recession, import barriers, export subsidies, and other forms of competition, as well as fluctuating prices, interest rates, currencies, and weather conditions. Instead many tend to receive high, protected incomes because in recent times governments have attracted many workers from the private sector, and because entry into the professions and trades is restricted—the long and costly education and/or apprenticeship involved, plus their non-competitive or even mandated fees, are things that internationally competitive industries cannot afford.

In contrast, the 50 percent of the Canadian labour force that is subject to international competition is directly vulnerable. In addition, it supports the whole economy, which is thereby indirectly vulnerable to all the above foreign competition and instability—although you would never know it from the guaranteed income security (for example, incomes and pensions indexed to inflation) that many of the 50 percent enjoy. Yet we do not make any special provisions for the vital and vulnerable export sector of our economy, even though we generously subsidize non-work.

We thus seem to shoot ourselves in the foot economically, partly because we have rejected or forgotten the insights of mercantilist analysis. As a result, our internationally competitive private sector has to become very productive, efficient, and competitive, very well paid, and ready to lay off many workers, replacing them with machines and computers. Then this competitive export sector is copied by the non-internationally competitive private industries and government. They all claim that they have to do the same to compete domestically and save money for the consumer and the taxpayer, using computerization and the latest in labour-saving technology to lay off workers.

In Canada and other countries blessed with major resource strength in gold, oil/gas and other commodities, we have been doing well until recently. But countries not so blessed, including the United States, have not been doing so well. Even in resource-based economies, where the resource-export sectors have become more internationally competitive than the domestic sectors, as in Canada and in Trinidad and Tobago, problems can arise from export wages becoming higher than domestic sector wages. Workers are drawn by the higher wages, making other industries uncompetitive and leading to more unemployment and higher inflation - and excluded workers and the homeless join the ranks of the poor.

What the mercantilist argument implies is that we should assist and not burden our internationally competitive exporting and import-competing sectors. We should do this rather than concentrate in a Keynesian way on running government deficits, increasing government spending and bank money supplies to artificially stimulate the dependent economy in an inflationary way that hurts our internationally competitive sectors. We then raise interest rates to fight inflation and support the dollar, and depress our internationally competitive sectors. Thus we dangerously damage our export lifeline, as mercantilist analysis stresses. (However, when our import-competing industries land in trouble, we change our minds on interest rates, regardless of inflation dangers.)

Prosperity can last as long as the U.S. and world economies remain peaceful and buoyant and open to our trade surpluses, and while we remain competitive and successful at selling our export surpluses. We cannot count on this, but we can do our best in a mercantile way by assisting our export industries, distributing and diversifying the proceeds widely, and increasing productivity. Thereafter, while the economy is buoyant we can finance other, neglected needs, such as by fighting poverty, overcoming debt, and tackling the environmental crisis.

Investment Implications

Canada is very dependent on resource exports to an unstable and sometimes warlike world economy. Therefore the Canadian dollar's value depends largely upon the strength (volume and value) of these resource exports (and on foreign investment attracted to them). If the strength is good, the Canadian dollar tends to rise vis à vis the U.S. dollar; if not, it tends to fall. Meanwhile, at least two of these resources—gold and oil—tend to rise both in good times and in bad. Accordingly, investors holding Canadian dollars pretty well cannot lose by investing in *Canadian dividend-paying gold and oil resource export stocks* (a high dollar when the price is high).[11] As a hedge and for income purposes, *short-term Canadian monetary assets* make sense, since they cannot lose much in Canadian dollar value, and they provide some income and are reasonably safe against both moderate inflation and moderate deflation. *Gold and silver coins* are a useful backup against monetary disasters and almost certain inflation. The longer-term outlook under bank money, which is backed by nothing and increasing exponentially in volume for at least the past fifty years of inflation towards worthlessness, suggests not only gold and silver but also *land and real estate*, including productive land, if you can afford and look after them, plus your own home in any case (or more gold and silver if you cannot afford a home). *Income* is problematic, but dividend-paying resource stocks, bank stocks, short-term monetary assets, and real estate plus your own home can earn or save some income. *Cash* is also very desirable, for liquidity and security. These conclusions are summarized below:

- a little cash
- gold and silver bullion or coins
- dividend-paying gold and oil resource export stocks
- bank stocks, to go along with soaring money supplies (gold for inflation)
- short-term Canadian monetary assets (for income as well as liquidity)

- your own home, and maybe land and/or real estate, including productive land
- sources of water and energy (ecologically important)

Government and Mercantilism

Economic theorists, other than mercantilists and students of development and poverty alleviation, seem to spend a lot of time talking about (adequate) demand and little time discussing supply, that is, how increased output, investment, competitiveness, exports, and non-inflationary employment are to be brought about, or how individuals can be helped to help themselves. It is a relief, therefore, to find the Ontario government tackling this problem with a long list of "supporting and promoting functions" for supply development[12]:

1. Assistance and encouragement to private productive enterprise
   - subsidies
   - tax incentives
   - finance
   - insurance
   - protection
   - research
   - advice, extension, management, counselling

2. Provision and improvement of the economic infrastructure
   - transport and communications
     (a) Department of Highways
     (b) Ontario Northland Transportation Commission

- power and water
  (a) Hydro-Electric Power Commission of Ontario
  (b) Ontario Water Resources Commission

3. Provision and improvement of the social infrastructure
   - Ministry of Education: technical and vocational manpower development
   - Ministry of Labour: industrial training program
   - Ministry of Agriculture: agricultural education and extension
   - other departmental and technical training facilities

4. Opening up, conservation, and development of natural resources
   - roads to resources
   - mineral and forest surveys
   - development and conservation of forests, fisheries and wildlife
   - increasing agricultural output and productivity

5. Industrial development and trade expansion: need for expansion of research in and assistance to the manufacturing sector, and studies of the construction, financial, and other service sectors
   - attracting foreign investment
   - promoting import replacement
   - assisting and encouraging export expansion

- other industrial promotion services
- development and promotion of tourism

6. Maintaining a high level of employment and demand

Compared with Ontario's detailed approach, the federal programs seem sparse, but powerful. They are more concerned with constitutional powers of finance and external trade, including in the latter the traditional mercantilist functions of export promotion, external trade offices, export credits, influence over interest rate and exchange rate policies, drawback programs (such as removal of the GST on exported goods), negotiations of treaties of commerce such as free trade agreements, and import restrictions. The last of these lay down tariff rates for our free-trade partners and for Most Favoured Nations. There are favourable tariffs for a few small developing countries,[13] and for all others much higher tariffs, plus schedules of quotas and embargoes on goods from non-favoured nations and enemies. All these are pure mercantilist policies.

Mercantilism and Simcoe County

The model in Figure 5 (below) is based on data from Simcoe County, Ontario. It applies to regions and countries that cannot create and expand their own money supplies or run large government deficits. This model maintains that the equilibrium size of the economy (national or regional income) is determined essentially by the money brought in by exports and other receipts from outside (for example, labour remittances), multiplied by the number of times that money is kept circulating domestically before it leaks abroad (non-market or non-monetary activities also add to "income," but are not counted here). The money from outside stimulates the local economy; redistribution and diversification by dependent industries and government multiply total income; and maintaining competitiveness keeps the economy going.

It is misleading to imagine that we can "print our way to riches" forever, even though some metropolitan nations have been able to get richer temporarily by doing so, along with their mercantilist activities, for some time. Poverty cannot be printed into riches; instead, governments and business leaders and skilled workers must produce, and then find export markets for their industries' products to stimulate their economy in a real and sustainable manner. They must distribute, widely circulate, and diversify the proceeds and multiply the benefits in the home market, then increase productivity and output through investments to remain competitive, improve conditions, and provide the extra means to tackle dispossessed poverty, overhanging debts, environmental degradation, and other problems that are being tackled by the welfare state, monetary theorists, ecologists, and so on.

In a regional economy without its own central bank to authorize the creation of local money, and in small national economies unable to create independent currencies, money consists of outside incomes flowing in, then circulating locally or nationally until they leak away to people and firms outside the regional or national economy, as in Figure 4. The local economy soon reaches an "equilibrium" level of income and employment in accordance with its exports: money inflows and outflows are the same. The only way to increase income and employment and to alleviate poverty in such areas (without balance of payments deficits or devaluation) is to increase production and sales of exports and import substitutes.

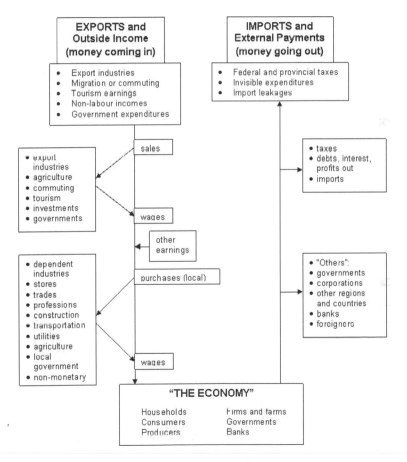

Figure 5: How a regional economy works, showing the flow of income.

In such regions and small nations, monetary and fiscal (macro) policies do not enter into consideration—there is no central bank and little ability to borrow and run a deficit—and Keynesian policy ideas are thus irrelevant. *Only mercantilist analysis applies.* Local economies depend on local and outside entrepreneurs and investors creating enterprises to produce exports and to replace imports, using local workers; on local labour's earning outside income by commuting or "migrating"; and often especially on foreign investment, because local credit-granting facilities and creditworthiness may be inadequate. Foreign investment that creates exports is almost always welcome. Programs to assist these creators of economic activity, and the workers carrying out the activity, can be of great importance in development and poverty-alleviation programs.

Simcoe County's Development Experience

The economic history of Simcoe County shows a clear example of mercantilist or staple export-led development. In the seventeenth and eighteenth centuries the principal market activity of white people in this area was fur trading (for export) with resident Natives. Large-scale European settlement began in the nineteenth century, and one of the earliest important industries in the county was lumbering (for export), which was facilitated from 1853 onwards by the arrival of railways (a directly productive infrastructure activity, or DPA, to facilitate exports). The small villages along the rail lines became shipping centres (another DPA) for lumber and agricultural products. Small local industries sprang up in these villages, including facilities for grain milling and cheese making (both for import substitution and for export), as well as the larger industry of shipbuilding (for export).

Towards the end of the nineteenth century, agriculture started to become more mechanized and diversified from mainly grain to livestock, dairying, and pork (export) production. From that time up until the 1950s, agriculture was the dominant industry in Simcoe County. Now, however, it is the least important major industry. More recently, industrial and commercial service development and professions (import substitute and export) has expanded, especially in Barrie. Tourism and commuting to Toronto (both export activities) are challenging the service industries as to which is the fastest-growing sector, except in periods of economic slowdown, when unemployment insurance, pensions, non-wage incomes, and welfare (all exports—that is, dollars coming into the region from senior governments and outside corporations) combine to become the largest source of outside income (an interesting example of rural and regional development, which is discussed in chapter 4).

Simcoe County has thus rapidly become a diversified, export-led-plus-import-substitute-multiplied economy, characterized by market (private enterprise) development with government infrastructure and social support, plus urbanization of the rural economy and features of rural and regional development (e.g., clusters of small firms around an established industry that brings in outside money). Alongside the above export industries, the region has developed communities of various sizes and rural and regional service centres that now house and service most of the region's population (a large part of which is urbanized). These centres provide practically all the new jobs, which are of course dependent on money brought in by the export industries.

Therefore the region's formerly rural, largely self-sufficient economy has now become overlaid by modern industries that employ specialized workers. These workers produce for outside markets and live mostly in urban areas connected by roads, railways, telecommunications, and the cash nexus. They are dependent on outside markets, banks, and governments and are "monetarily expanded" by social benefits income. The region exhibits little visible change except in the expanding urban areas and in strip malls and housing estates along the roads. It continues to look primarily rural, but its people's livelihoods are now mostly non-agricultural and non-self-sufficient—dependent on exports to the outside economy, as the mercantilists describe. It has not developed, and would not have been able to develop, through agriculture alone.[14]

Mercantilism and the L0L1P0 Small Farm Experiment

To further study and test my ideas about what supply measures to take to lessen rural (and related urban) poverty, I began an experiment—a small farm called L0L1P0, after its postal code—in Simcoe County in 1974. The main idea behind that move was to supplement my theoretical studies of agriculture, economics, and economic development with practical experience of a commercial small farm operation, and to write up my findings and conclusions in a way that could be useful later.

For example, here are four related general findings:

1. Successful rural development is very difficult to achieve through agricultural (supply) development alone, except in large units or cooperative/joint units for export.
2. Successful small-farm rural development requires non-agricultural or "balanced" (demand) rural and regional development as well, as in diversification around an export base in the staple theory and in the large agricultural demonstration projects illustrated in chapter 4.
3. As regards individual farms, intensification of output (per acre) on already settled land may be necessary, possible, and desirable in order to promote rural development and keep people from migrating to the cities (see chapter 4), but complete self-sufficiency is almost impossible except

in primitive or isolated cases. (Intensification also depends on resources such as soil and water, and on investments/credit.)

4. Intensification may require smaller-acreage farms and different technology. This, in turn, may require credit and land reform.

A fascinating thing about dividing up large farms into smaller units is that this can increase values (both utilitarian and financial) and liquidity. It is an open secret locally that, if you can get the local government to approve a subdivision on your land, the land will increase in value per acre—additional wealth will have been created out of nothing! When a bank lends you money in exchange for the deed on your house, it creates liquid assets (money) out of nothing. These assets are acceptable, convertible, and valuable and can buy other things, so you have more money and the bank has more wealth (your debt, property deed, etc.). Similarly, if the Royal Canadian Mint stamps a premium face value on a gold coin and the government guarantees that value as legal tender, they create extra liquidity or premium value by making that stamped gold coin liquid, acceptable, and convertible into more money than the value of the gold alone, with no extra material and little extra labour.

Suppose, in a program of land reform, the government takes over a 100-acre farm with $100,000 of newly created money borrowed from a bank, (Now 100-acre farms are selling for

$1,000,000 and more, away from cities!) and subdivides it into ten 10-acre lots. It sells these to a developer for $150,000 to be "developed" with roads, water supply, electricity, and so on at an additional cost of $50,000. Then the developer sells the land for a total price of $250,000 to ten small farmers, who borrow that new money for the purchase from the bank, against their equity in the developed land. The developer then pays off its loan from the bank. Extra value and production potential have been created several times over, out of nothing except the undeveloped liquidity, productivity, and convenience of the land. Very quickly, more economic value has been created than the new small farmers could match over many years! If this is indeed economic development, why should any government say it does not have enough money to promote land reform? An interesting monetary thought, indeed.

I bought my L0L1P0 homestead with borrowed bank money from a large-scale farmer. (He had just severed my 4¼ acres of good farm land with its house and barn, and sold it to me for about as much as his 100 acres had cost him previously.) I paid it off by selling other assets used to back my loan, and settled down to intensify this small acreage (which was now worth much more because of investments and inflation).

I put in advanced facilities for egg-laying poultry, buying the chickens and feed from larger-scale farms and farm-supply cooperatives, and "adding value" to my small acreage as if it were

Figure 6: Aerial view of the L0L1P0 experiment, Simcoe County, Ontario.

a factory. That is, I housed the chickens, fed, watered, and cleaned them, and collected, washed, candled, graded, packed, and sold the eggs. I carefully cultivated vegetables on a market-garden scale rather than pursuing an extensive grain or cattle operation, and I planned how to market both types of produce—by demand creation as well as by supply expansion. For the vegetables I reached an agreement with a local supermarket to deliver fresh, presentable, organic vegetable produce daily in season. The store already had an egg supplier, so I peddled my eggs to households daily by truck, knowing that if I expanded my output I would have to sell it to the Ontario Egg Marketing Board at a slightly lower per unit price (under a "supply management" program designed (by me) to prevent surpluses, collapsing prices, failed enterprises, poverty, wasted capital, and future high prices).

With backbreaking labour and sixteen-hour days (plus family help), the experiment earned—through developing supply and demand—more than $30,000 (gross) per year in 1974 Canadian dollars. This would be more now with higher prices—eggs having practically quadrupled in price in the interim—but my example invited competition in the limited local market. On a larger scale I would now have to "export" the eggs to the Ontario Egg Marketing Board and the vegetables to Barrie and/or Toronto, requiring a bigger operation and higher costs. These details show that, with land, much labour, and capital (much more than is commonly suggested by aid agencies), small farm development is possible and viable as a basis for poverty-relieving development. But it is not possible unless all the requirements (described in my book *Trying to Help*) are fully met—this is not child's play, and it is not possible without skills and/or assistance.

Although such an experience would not be exactly the same in its details in a particular poor country, region, or "reserve," I hoped that its findings would in principle seem relevant to others, and would even help in the alleviation of poverty in some areas. Here are two of those findings:

- Production problems are often easier to solve than marketing problems, given adequate resources and people able to offer both credit and practical advice. You need initial help from farmers or agricultural extension officers who know what they are doing, backup money or credit sources, and good relations with the local people to get things going and keep things working. And then you have to solve marketing problems . . .

- You need to solve marketing or sales problems because you can't get far with self-sufficiency. This is particularly difficult if the surrounding region and country are not prosperous enough (from exports) to provide strong local demand. It may also be difficult if markets are too far away, or if there are too many producers competing for a limited local market, that is, too much local supply not being sold abroad. In other words, what is desirable to help development in an undeveloped area is development, practical action, and problem solving, particularly through exports—and preferably in a balanced, diversified way—the mercantilist prescription. You have to move from practically nothing to actual production, marketing, and profits through hard work and sales, not through gifts or aid. And you have to carve out money-buying markets the mercantilist way before you can expand to tackle poverty.

What made the L0L1P0 experiment feasible was that the region (Simcoe County) was prosperous (it had people and firms with money who would buy) because of strong exports from mercantilistic development dating way back. This had brought outside money into the region and created a helpful situation of prosperity and high local demand. An additional aid was that commuting to Toronto, a source of alternative employment and high opportunity costs for many local workers, made local small-scale farming relatively unrewarding to local labour, so local markets welcomed local produce (with money from exports). But if such favourable local market conditions do not apply, how can one develop markets for one's new produce? Here are two suggestions:

- the specialized commercial way, in which one produces, processes, transports, and sells—or has some organization perform those functions, such as the Egg Marketing Board— that is, one exports commodities to faraway metropolitan and/or export markets. Such exporting may initially seem to be beyond the capabilities of small farmers and small businesses, but here is where cooperative or corporate sales organizations or local sales outlets (such as an egg-grading station) may come in.
- using organizations set up to collect and export, whose services include advertising, processing, transport, and some integration. These organizations are planned and set up for exporting to wider and more distant markets. They offer greater sales efforts and new and improved types and qualities of products, such as more processed or preserved products—jam instead of fruit, or growing fruits to use one's sugar production with or vice versa. Some excellent government-sponsored organizations exist to perform these functions, even on a national scale.

With the L0L1P0 experiment and these marketing investigations, I was learning-by-doing economic development myself and hoping to pass on some lessons to others. My general conclusions were that (a) monetary manipulation (demand creation and redistribution) alone cannot solve economic development and poverty alleviation (supply and marketing) problems, and (b) real experience supports the mercantile thesis that linking to the outside export market seems practically essential for development and poverty alleviation. You have to have the resources, the people, the capital, the understanding of what is necessary, and the willingness and ability to work. Then, if you can get an export operation going, other small enterprises can gather around it to start a village (i.e., rural and regional development), keep people in the rural areas, and as a result reduce poverty, starting in the rural districts, then spreading to the urban areas. (A local farm family expanded their fruit and dairy farms to add a local farm supplies store and a post office, greatly increasing their local employment and value-added!).

Mercantilism and South Africa

South Africa was a mercantilist white-ruled colony originally conquered by the imperial power to secure its gold, with several "hinterlands" housing most of its African labour. It is now an independent black-ruled country that includes several desperately poor rural hinterlands that supply substantial (40 to 50 percent unemployed) "exports" of labour to the metropolitan centres (plus about 20 million unemployed refugees), which are in turn largely dependent on exports of gold and other resources. The country was, and is, a mercantile creation—resource exports, imports of manufactures, import substitutes around the export base, then a series of incentives to help it grow—with large-scale great wealth amid pockets of poverty. It needs the mercantilist remedies of export promotion, import substitution, and diversification, as well as policies to increase productivity and competitiveness and help it grow. As argued below, it also needs some important monetary reforms (parallel gold-backed commodity money) to reduce enormous unemployment and poverty, without inflation, and to lessen suffering in both rural and urban slums, along with planned rural development. (Chapters 2 and 5 show that these reforms are also needed to prevent future monetary collapse.)

The desperately poor hinterlands—the former "native reserves"—came into being when the native peoples were dispossessed of good land and pushed back onto inadequate marginal lands. They then overpopulated and severely depleted their limited land resources, and, unable to support themselves on their land, crowded into the cities (and onto white-owned farms) to look for work in the invading economic culture. However, they remained heavily unemployed and poor even there. Severe poverty and disease (and other problems) became endemic to both "reserve" and urban migrant populations and to black labour on white farms. In addition, as explained further below, the national government and the central bank could not create sufficient money demand to employ all these migrants for fear of generating inflation, then devaluation, then hyperinflation and ultimately "failed state" conditions. They needed the parallel gold-backed commodity money solution described in chapter 2.

Even when the Africans gained political control over South Africa and its homelands, they could not do much to develop and alleviate poverty in the reserves and in the satellite settlements in the metropoles. This was because the reserves lacked the resources—land, minerals, capital, fertile soil, water (which had been captured by the whites)—to develop strong exports to support massive populations on minimal land; and because the resulting migrants did not have prosperous city jobs (because of monetary problems discussed later) that would enable them to send sufficient money back home. Thus income also remained inadequate until reverse mercantilist flows could be increased.

The overcrowded, eroded rural slums had nothing attractive to develop, so there seemed no alternative to continued flight from these moonscapes into the overcrowded, unemployed, criminal, diseased city slums. However, two mercantilistic developments helped. One was migrant labour, or "export" sales of their remaining resource, labour; the other was political rescue in the form of incoming receipts ("exports") of wages and benefits from the new, African-led government.

I tried to work out solutions to this type of poverty through improved agriculture (my agriculture degree, the L0L1P0 experiment, recommendations of more land for the Africans, papers outlining plans for rural and regional development, descriptions of reverse mercantilism). Marxism, socialism, and Keynesianism were useless because there was nothing to take, nothing to redistribute (within the reserves), and nothing to stimulate. But something might be worked out through reverse mercantilism and parallel commodity money.

Every economic unit, whether an individual, a family, a farm, a region, or a country, has its equilibrium income determined by the value of its exports multiplied by the number of times export dollars circulate locally before leaking abroad, plus self-sufficient, non-traded production value. This can be expressed as a formula:

equilibrium $Y \leq E/m$ plus self-sufficient (non-monetary) output,

where $\quad Y$ = national or regional income

$\quad\quad\quad E$ = exports

$\quad\quad\quad m$ = the fraction of income (Y) spent on imports (M)

and $\quad\quad E \leq M = mY$

This formula expresses numerically what the mercantilists say. We can see that, if income is artificially stimulated by increases in the money supply or government deficits, imports (M) will come to exceed exports (E). The result will be balance-of-payments deficits, depreciation in the exchange-rate valuation of the dollar, inflation and more balance-of-payments deficits, and so on, until money loses value and hyperinflationary chaos sets in. Or, if money is not created locally, the cycle will continue until money leaks out and the economy shrinks to almost nothing unless restrictive monetary and fiscal policies are introduced—leading to recession, higher unemployment, more poverty, and a dead economy unless expansionary policies are introduced again, leading to hyperinflationary chaos . . . and so on (or unless non-Keynesian export expansion is achieved).[15]

Therefore, Keynesian deficit-financing policies to fight unemployment and poverty will (eventually) not work, and governments will have to impose restrictive policies to prevent runaway inflation, even though such policies cause high unemployment and severe poverty. Governments such as South Africa's will have to maintain severe unemployment and poverty unless they can go the mercantilist way and expand exports or introduce a parallel commodity money. This can be done only if the parallel, backed currency does not lose value as in the case of inflation of non-backed bank money, as explained in chapter 2. Only then can lasting poverty be remedied. Such remedies would provide indirect aid to the reserves by increasing the number of jobs and the level of wages for migrant workers, thus enabling them to send back more "export" money to the reserves (reverse mercantilism). Given this start, the prospects for planned rural development become brighter and planned development becomes more feasible.

Mercantilism and the Native Reserves

While the above theses (reverse mercantilism, parallel commodity money, and balanced rural and regional development) embody this book's principal recommendations, a more down-to-earth description is nevertheless necessary for fuller understanding of the problem of poverty. Therefore we now turn to a couple of brief looks at life in the native reserves of South Africa.

It was as a schoolboy in 1949 that I first looked out at the surrounding "native reserve" from Emsebeni, our house at the top of the hill on Adams Mission Station in KwaZulu Natal, South Africa. Native reserves were segregated rural areas, many in number that comprised about 13 percent of the total land area of South Africa. They were intended to be the "homelands" of Africans, who made up about 75 percent of the population. Whites, 15 percent of the population, owned nearly 87 percent of the land. Thus the whites had about thirty-three times as much land per person than the Africans,[16] ($87/15 \div 13/75 = 87/15$ x $75/13 = 33.46$) plus almost all the resources, including gold, platinum and diamond mines, all the cities, industries, and infrastructures, and most of the capital, skills, and well-paid jobs. This discrimination and inequality were joint major causes of poverty in South Africa.

I resolved to do something about that problem. In 1955 I did some research work on the reserve surrounding the mission station, which was near Durban, for a master of science degree in agriculture. This survey work revealed that the overcrowded, eroded, third-rate land, which had been abandoned by the active labour force, produced almost nothing. This was partly a cause and partly an effect of the fact that the working-age population could earn more (than almost nothing) in the white-run cities. Therefore they left the land and migrated, supposedly temporarily, to the cities to earn some "export" money to send back to support those still in the reserves (much as in Simcoe County). For instance, one "farm" I visited had one chicken running loose, three goats eating anywhere, and an unkempt "garden" that produced almost nothing. The children were in Durban; there were no fences, no electricity, no water, wells, or pens; and the old folk were simply "residents" in the country, although better off than most because they were living on minute pensions.[17]

Alan Paton, in *Cry, the Beloved Country*, described this tragedy of poverty and discrimination in beautiful language:

> There is a lovely road that runs from Ixopo into the hills. These hills are grass-covered and rolling and they are lovely beyond any singing of it. The road climbs seven miles into them, to Carisbrooke; and from there, if there is no mist, you look down on one of the fairest valleys of Africa. About you there is grass and bracken and you may hear the forlorn crying of the titihoya, one of the birds of the veld. The grass is rich and matted, you cannot see the soil. It holds the rain and the mist, and they seep into the ground, feeding the streams in every kloof. It is well-tended, and not too many cattle feed upon it; not too many

fires burn it, laying bare the soil. Stand unshod upon it, for the ground is holy, being even as it came from the Creator. Keep it, guard it, care for it, for it keeps men, guards men, cares for men. Destroy it and man is destroyed.

Where you stand the grass is thick and matted, you cannot see the soil. But the rich green hills break down. They fall to the valley below, and falling, change their nature. For they grow red and bare; they cannot hold the rain and the mist, and the streams are dry in the kloofs. Too many cattle feed upon the grass, and too many fires have burned it. Stand shod upon it, for it is coarse and sharp, and the stones cut under the feet. It is not kept, or guarded, or cared for, it no longer keeps men, guards men, cares for men. The titihoya does not cry here any more.

The great red hills stand desolate, and the earth has torn away like flesh. The lightning flashes over them, the clouds pour down upon them, the dead streams come to life, full of the red blood of the earth. Down in the valleys, women scratch the soil that is left, and the maize hardly reaches the height of a man. They are valleys of old men and old women, of mothers and children. The men are away, the young men and the girls are away. The soil cannot keep them any more.[18]

Figure 7: South Africa—young thorn bush growing on severely eroded land (Source: Houghton and Walton)

These word-pictures show the resident Africans' initial answer to a poverty that was initiated by mercantilist land-grabs and perpetuated by apartheid. Apartheid decreed that Africans weren't allowed to "immigrate" to live permanently on white land in the white cities, and only as landless labourers on white farms. Instead they migrated to "temporary" shacks near where the jobs and money were—in the cities—exporting their only exportable asset, their labour, in order to send some money back home to the reserves. There the outside money circulated briefly, supporting the trading posts—the only local economic activity other than local self-sufficiency and barter—before their families leaked it out (spent it on imports) at the Indian or White trading posts. Then trading activity died to almost nothing. This mercantilistic rural economic picture (rich metropolis, poor hinterland) is still largely true under African rule today, more than fifty years later.

A more detailed description of a native reserve and reverse mercantilism—in which poverty caused by mercantilism from outside is partly answered by reverse mercantilism from within (export of labour for survival)—may be obtained from *The Economy of a Native Reserve*, by D. Hobart Houghton and Edith M. Walton. The authors describe one such reserve: "The Keiskammahoek Native Reserve, in the Eastern Cape Province of South Africa, consists of a small, 220 square mile pocket of rough land, marked off for 'Natives' by the invading White settlers around 1853."[19]

Land was the basic resource sought, mercantilistically or imperialistically, by both whites and Africans, and the Africans were dispossessed of most of their land by the European military. Before European expropriation, the Africans were largely self-sufficient, as well as being exporters of ivory, hides and skins, and wool. After expropriation, the remaining Africans were grouped into "native reserves" that were totally inadequate as a resource or home base. In the mid-twentieth century the general characteristics of the reserves were "overpopulation, overstocking, denudation of the vegetation (deforestation), soil erosion and poverty,"[20] plus low productivity, large-scale emigration, and "migration," or temporary commuting to jobs in the cities for varying periods of time.

"The land [was] unable to support its population" of around 18,000 people.[21] Accordingly, the Africans had to export their principal resource (labour) to get money to buy imports, the local "dormitory suburb" economy being almost dead. Attempts were being made to "develop" these reserves in order to keep the Africans *apart*. The Africans were answering these attempts in a reverse mercantilistic way by exporting their labour and their populations to the cities, where conditions were atrocious and unemployment was in the range of 40 to 50 percent. In chapter 2 I suggest the use of parallel commodity money to enable the national economy to provide more employment in order to alleviate poverty in the urban monetary economy without hyperinflation. After that beginning, more money might come from the cities to develop the desolate reserves, and perhaps even to buy more land through a land reform program.

The point I want to stress is that reverse mercantilism plus parallel commodity money was the only way out, as in the small West Indian islands discussed below. This was a *survival* strategy; the Africans are still poor, but reverse mercantilism allows them to live.

Mercantilism in Trinidad and Tobago

Trinidad and Tobago were captured by a succession of European colonizers and settled in order to grow plantation crops such as sugar, cocoa, coffee, and copra, using slaves, then indentured labourers. Subsequent events, spurred by the oil and gas industry, were not specifically mercantilistic, but the closing down of many agricultural estates because of high oil-fed wages suggests that estate labour had been previously underpaid (cheap resources and cheap labour). And overcharging by protected assembly industries suggests that foreign firms were exploiting the islands' economy.

Early on, Trinidad was blessed with substantial oil discoveries (some on my family's cocoa estate![22]). At the outset, oil exports provided some high-paid jobs for oil workers, plus plentiful revenue for the government with which to employ civil servants and provide welfare and low-level jobs and stimulate the economy. In addition, U.S. dollar inflows from outside supported the currency and enabled some to live well—indeed, much better than before. But these higher incomes were too much for almost every industry other than oil and gas (except the highly protected import-substitute assembly plants discussed below) and led people to expect the easy life and to disdain "slave labour" work such as cutting sugar cane. As a result, unemployment and imports soared, the currency started to decline, prices started rising, and, about a half-century later, economic conditions were described as being worse for many than in the neighbouring non-oil-rich, lower-income islands, which had lower prices and less inflation.

Then came import substitution. Given high wages, a strong currency (still supported by oil export revenues), high unemployment, and mostly uncompetitive industries producing internationally traded products, plus growing imports and eventual balance-of-payments deficits, Trinidad's manufacturers argued for protection—and they got it, to ridiculous levels. Import substitution was the solution, so some clever people persuaded the government to let them assemble cars in Trinidad, with an import duty of 25 percent on fully manufactured cars and none on imported components.[23] No less than three modern auto plants, with assembly lines and skilled workers, were set up in this small, poor island to serve the protected local market. New jobs, modern manufacturing, and reduced imports resulted. How could anyone complain about this move into the industrial age?

The trouble was that the cost of the imported components that escaped the tariff, according to the accountant at one of the factories, was 97 percent of the value of an imported assembled car before duty, producing only a 3 percent saving in import costs per car. This meant that the 3 percent assembly operation was protected by a margin of 833 percent! (25/3 x 100%) [24] This was far more (perhaps a hundred times more) than any existing industry would have needed in order to compete in export or import-substitute production. The government had to raise taxes and reduce spending (i.e., jobs) because of lost import duties, and the prices of these protected goods did not decline, while more competitive industries went under.

> The assembly plants were so inefficient (or so profitable or transferred so much money abroad) that, if every other industry was equally inefficient, prices would have gone up 833 percent. Incomes would have fallen to a fraction of their former purchasing power before hyperinflation set in. The problem was an overvalued exchange rate, given the higher income levels and

resulting higher price levels due to oil, which were maintained to avoid inflationary harm to those with money (who might move it abroad and bring down the currency) and to those with wages (who could not have afforded the higher cost of living), and to reduce the closing of many formerly competitive industries, which were suffering from wage hikes. This overvalued exchange rate led to highly protected, inefficient import-substitute assembly plants. It made it impossible for Trinidad to expand import substitutes or non-oil exports, and thus employ its population, stimulate its economy, and support its currency. The island nation became massively unemployed and politically riven, exporting desperate "economic refugees" (a reverse mercantilistic tactic) both despite and because of the wealth brought to some by oil. The only solution I could think of, besides the eventual, inevitable devaluation (or collapse when the oil ran out), might have been to use the oil windfall to invest in, even subsidize, new industries and productivity increases, which might have increased exports and employment without subsequent devaluation.[25] (I lived through mercantilistic cocoa estates, imperialistic oil discoveries, superior missionary stations, racist apartheid, attempts to find export promotion and import substitution remedies, economic refugees due to oil, criticism for being too mercantilistic therefore failed Ph. D, and other attempts to help culminating in this book).

Mercantilism and Reverse Mercantilism in Grenada, St. Kitts, and Zimbabwe

As requested by their respective high commissioners in Ottawa, in a paper written in November 2000 I described the economic predicaments of Grenada, St. Kitts, and Zimbabwe and tried to suggest some—largely mercantilistic—export solutions.[26] The first descriptive summary was headed "Colonial Past and Poverty-Stricken Present." In sum this meant that mercantilism plus imperialism plus colonialism plus capitalism had led to the creation of empires with plantations and slave labour in the colonies exporting raw materials to the motherland. After the slaves were freed, populations exploded and land reforms proceeded, but raw material prices remained low and soils became eroded and exhausted. These previous colonies became unprofitable and poverty-stricken and were largely abandoned by their colonizers. Mercantilism became redefined as exploiting cheap labour and resources until they were played out, then abandoning them and putting up tariffs against them.

Even in the new millennium I was still thinking in conventional terms, stressing agricultural development and not thinking outside the box in reverse mercantilistic terms. When I do the latter, I think of what else could be exported other than agricultural products from crowded, exhausted soils. As with the South African native reserves, I think of (a) emigration of significant parts of the population; (b) temporary labour migration to earn money to send back home; and (c) "exporting" parts of the land (its "services," such as climate and beaches) in the form of tourism and "tropical paradise" settlements, as in Florida. (Of course, these facilities could get bought up by foreigners.) In these ways islanders can get around the tariffs erected against them. (But tourism can become so profitable that, as in the Dutch Disease predicament, local agriculture becomes uncompetitive and almost all food is imported!)

Reporter Ruth Glass wrote an article from Jamaica in 1961 titled "The Inescapable Urge to Escape from the Carefree Islands." The setting was the docks of Kingston's harbour, where emigrants were piling aboard a crowded ship bound for London and other cities, six hundred at a time. They must go, they say, to find work and join relatives abroad. They must go soon, before immigration is restricted: it's "now or never." Jamaica's people suffer from a growing surplus of population. "The black masses exist [in the lowlands], in and around the appalling shack regions in an intolerable state of destitution, of blight, chaos and neglect [and crime]."[27] They must get out, to improve their lot and to send money back home. Jamaica is so unequal: from tourist resorts and rich mountain playgrounds along the north coast to eroded cane lands and landless poverty (I have seen enormous erosion gullies, perhaps fifty feet in depth, and goats denuding the surrounding land so that it falls into the gullies—right next to the University of the West Indies!) to city slums and the hellholes of Kingston. The situation is so bad that now a quarter of a million Jamaicans live in Toronto, and many more live in

New York, London, and other better-off cities. This is one side of reverse mercantilism, the other side being the flow of money "back home." It comes from early mercantilism plus slavery, exhaustion of the soil, subsequent freedom from slavery, and abandonment of the colonies. But this reverse mercantilism is problematic too, even if life-saving.

CHAPTER 2

Monetary Theory Reform

Confidence Money and (Parallel) Commodity Money Explained

In my 1996 book *Canada Savings Coins*, I proposed the introduction of a parallel, gold-containing commodity money as a savings vehicle alongside the existing, unbacked bank money. The basic idea was to remedy the inability of the unbacked bank-money system to protect savings against inflation, and to reduce inflation in ways that do not cause recession, unemployment, and poverty. Specifically, the argument was that little can be done through monetary and fiscal policy to reduce poverty in nations where the currency is unbacked bank money. This was because, if monetary and fiscal policies were expansionary or stimulative, inflation would accelerate, the balance of payments would deteriorate, devaluation would threaten, and inflation would rise further towards hyperinflationary collapse—a vicious circle. But when these policies had to become restrictive, recession and rising unemployment would ensue, moving towards depression. Thus, if a country with unbacked money faced severe unemployment and poverty, as many poor countries do, it could not solve these problems by using stimulative policies. Instead it would have to be restrictively cautious, and poverty would persist. Therefore, I argued, a new, parallel commodity-money system with a parallel, stable, gold-backed currency was necessary to fight inflation and to allow poor nations to expand and thus to gain a means of reducing poverty caused by unbacked bank money (we are here moving on from mercantilism-caused poverty).

The purpose of this parallel gold-backed currency would be to provide a stable, real-value, convertible currency savings vehicle. If the circulating bank money began to lose value or was expected to lose value, people could put their savings into this stable-value, gold-backed parallel currency in order to protect them against inflation, instead of having to put their money into inflation-hedge cost-of-living assets, pushing up the latters' prices and thereby *accelerating* inflation. Inflation could thus be reduced and the policymakers' fears that stimuli would produce runaway inflation and chaos could be alleviated. Limited inflation could continue and be adjusted to, aided by the value-preserving gold coins, without destroying people's savings. Following from this,

- savings would be protected;
- inflation would be reduced;
- jobs could be created, both by overall non-inflationary expansion and by the new industry producing and handling the gold coins;
- extra resources could be provided for social, economic, and environmental investments, such as rural and regional development, from the profits of this industry;
- the country would be saved from economic, monetary, and political collapse; and
- poverty could be reduced and alleviated!

The aim of my previous book was to achieve the above goals by introducing a premium real-value, money-guaranteed, gold-containing or intrinsically "backed" coin. This coin would be sold so that it could be in place in the event of an inflationary crisis, to operate parallel to the (inflationary) unbacked bank currency as a safe savings vehicle; it would have a guaranteed buy-back value in bank money as well as a real value in gold. The coin would have a legal tender or government-guaranteed cash value initially greater than its gold-content value, thus protecting against collapse and making the coin worth more at home than abroad. And by protecting savings against inflation as well as collapse, it would lessen people's anxious eagerness to invest in cost-of-living inflation-hedge assets or in capital flight, both of which increase the vicious circle of inflation, devaluation, more inflation, restrictive policies, depression, expansionary policies, renewed inflation, and so on.

The historical "hard money" argument[1] is that inflation leading to poverty has long been a scourge and a menace, a tragedy, and a problem desperately needing to be solved. Adam Smith argued that specialization and exchange (and a favourable balance of trade) would promote the wealth of nations and alleviate poverty by increasing productivity, amounts exchanged, and the domestic supply of money. However, even if his greater productivity and favourable balance of trade arguments hold, continuing poverty and repeated depressions have led most political economists to ask how such increasing outputs could continue to be sold (that is, to find demand or markets) so that the economy would not become depressed. To enable growing outputs to be sold, the mercantilists said, "Bring in more money [from the outside]"; the bankers said, "Create more money [internally]"; and Marx said "Take [surplus] money from the rich and give it to the workers," who would spend it all, thus maintaining employment. These three approaches were all aimed at generating adequate demand to prevent depression and poverty.

Much later on, in the midst of the Great Depression, Keynes said instead, "Don't confiscate [or tax] money from the rich, but borrow [run deficits] and create [lend more] money for the purpose of generating adequate demand." His prescription seemed to work wonders in the rich nations for several decades, but eventually the debts, inflation, balance-of-payments deficits, devaluations, and so on from all that borrowing and money creation began to wreak havoc. Governments and banking systems had to cut back, leading to a return of inadequate demand and contributing to unemployment and poverty. The Keynesian deficit-spending prescription began to be questioned because it led to the expectation of inflation—which speeded up inflation and its concomitant problems—and then to the expectation (and actuality) of restrictions/recession ahead—which speeded up deflation.

The leading thinkers had advocated productivity (Smith), exports and trade surpluses (mercantilism), confiscation (Marx), redistribution (socialism), and expanded money supplies and deficit spending (Keynes). These had all been tried but none had worked perfectly, and now there were new problems: devaluation, runaway inflation, restrictive policies, renewed unemployment, and growing inequality and poverty due both to fear of rising prices and to unemployment. We could not find a lasting and satisfactory solution to the problem of poverty—at least as long as we depended only on unbacked, ever-expanding bank money. One task of this book is thus to argue that at least a partial solution to the above problems could be found by creating and introducing a parallel, gold-backed commodity money. The World Bank did it for two and a half decades up to 1971—"hard money" is not so new.

But how did we come to depend on our unbacked, ever exponentially expanding bank money? Consider the following story. Early goldsmith bankers used to take in deposits of gold—an early form of money—for safekeeping, issuing in return receipts, IOUs, or banknotes that promised to pay the bearer, on demand (in exchange), a stated weight of gold. Since gold was an existing currency in which people had confidence, these 100 percent gold-backed notes eventually became accepted in trade and exchange as "confidence money," because people were confident that the notes were backed by and convertible into gold—as good as gold, in other words. Confidence was transferred from the gold to these convenient banknotes because people believed they could obtain gold, a widely accepted medium of exchange that would retain its value, in return for their paper.

When people had gained confidence in these 100 percent gold-backed bank notes and had largely stopped coming back to the banks to convert them into gold, the banks found that they had idle or "excess" reserves of gold. In their quest for maximum profits, they issued additional promissory (IOU gold) debt-money banknotes (which were actually fraudulent, because they promised to pay in gold they did not have or that was already promised to others) as loans to borrowers who put up securities other than gold; they had to borrow their IOU money *and* provide securities. This created more "debt money" bank IOUs for which the banks supposedly owned gold, and borrowers owed the banks borrowed "bank money," which is how they promised to repay the loan principal, plus interest, while the banks retained proof of ownership of the debt. (Remember that the banks did not have the gold to repay borrowers who brought back bank IOU money.) This established a situation where not all debts to the banks could be repaid with interest in bank money unless the supply of bank money was expanded exponentially—at least as fast as the average interest rate—leading to inflation and, eventually, worthless bank money!

The additional money was not backed by gold, and eventually *all* bank money came to be backed only by "fractional reserves" of gold, which today have diminished to practically nothing—in effect nothing, since the banks no longer promise to repay banknotes with gold, and only hold commercial or government money debts as backing for their bank-money debts.[2] Nevertheless, the additional banknotes became, alongside the original notes and deposits, acceptable in trade and exchange, as well as for saving, because people still had (false) confidence that they were convertible into gold at a fixed rate (the limited numbers of conversions in the early days tended to confirm that confidence).

When the fractional reserve system had become established, any scare such as a war or inflation (hence monetary policies whose only goal was to keep inflation down), or a rumour that there was not enough gold (which there wasn't), could lead to a "run on the banks." People could demand their gold, leading to exhaustion of reserves and realization that bank money was intrinsically worthless—not accepted and runaway inflationary. Banks would become "bankrupt" and currencies would collapse; "failed states," international conflict, and, of course, lasting mass poverty would ensue.

In response to these crises (or the danger of such crises), the major nations set up central banks to pool the remaining fractional reserves of the commercial banks into central bank (actual gold) "gold reserves." The central banks each issued powerful (promised gold) "reserve money," which was backed to a fraction of its value by the gold reserves. Deposits of this (fractional) reserve money were what the commercial banks had to hold as fractional reserves for their IOU bank money; thus bank money was "backed" by a fraction of a fraction of its value in gold. But eventually this farce was abandoned, bank money was secretly made unbacked by gold, and interest rates were supposed to control money supplies, inflation, and so on. The older ("gold standard") arrangement reduced the expansion of bank loan money in order to fight inflation; that later was found "inconvenient" and was secretly given up, but the abandonment was hardly noticed. All that presently gives bank money its value is its convertibility into other bank monies, rate of interest payable, and purchasing power. It's valuable because it's valuable.

Now the central bank sets an important "bank rate" to control the interest rate on chartered (commercial) bank borrowings of central bank reserve money to add to their own reserves, which "back" their unbacked bank loan money, the sum of which is the "money supply." Now you know why no one understands the money and banking system, and why inflation can easily get out of control, only to be checked by recession-causing high interest rates.

Now, when we have rising inflation, plummeting stocks, and soaring bankruptcies, no one seems to be asking about the value of our unbacked money (they are asking about the bank-money value of their other assets instead). This book does ask, and argues that lack of intrinsic value is the greatest threat to our monetary economy—a threat that can be defended against only by parallel commodity money.[3] Moreover, in private, but in expert circles, the idea that money has no value is gaining ground, and people are buying gold and other real assets instead.

Inflation continues, partly because interest on money lent by the banks, which is payable in addition to principal in the same bank money, means that not all debts to the banks can be repaid in full, with interest, in the same bank money, unless the bank-money supply is expanded exponentially (faster than the bank rate)—which it has been doing for at least the past fifty years (see Figure 8).

As a result of the above, after multiple hyperinflations, monetary crises, devaluations, and collapses/failed states, the Great Depression, the Second World War, and mass poverty problems linked directly or indirectly to these monetary crises, all nations eventually gave up on the gold standard; the United States waited until 1971 to do so. After going off gold, the world moved on to the U.S. dollar as a reserve currency—until Charles de Gaulle demanded gold in return for Frances' U.S. dollars and could not get it[4]—and then off reserves entirely and onto a sort of interest rate standard. This interest rate standard fights inflation (which would disprove the value of unbacked bank loan money) rather clumsily, by increasing the cost of money, thus threatening recession or depression (and worthless assets) in order to prevent bank money from becoming worthless through inflation. Then, frightened by asset deflation, central banks repeatedly slash interest rates, threatening runaway inflation through expanding money supplies. And, when that does not work, they bail out collapsing corporations with money backed by worthless assets . . .until it is realized that the central banks cannot cash out their debts with valuable assets, and the money backed by such assets loses value . . . Perhaps readers will now see why this book seeks a remedy through "real" parallel commodity money. Given the grave danger that we face, we will look at commodity money below after another important analytical view.

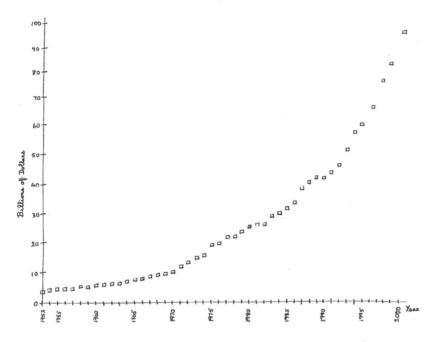

Figure 8: The Canadian M1 money supply, 1953 to 2007. Note the exponential acceleration in growth. (Source: Statistics Canada and Bank of Canada)

Monetary Policy: The Confidence/Convertibility Game

There are two broad reasons why government bank-money creation cannot alleviate poverty in poor counties. The first reason is that any bank-money creation, because it finances only those who are creditworthy and able to repay their loans with interest, by definition does not help the poor and un-creditworthy. Instead it facilitates the process whereby good land, resources, and business opportunities gravitate into the hands of the rich. And the rich seek to maximize profits with plantation agriculture, livestock estates, and sweatshop factories, driving most of the poor off the best land onto marginal hillsides and infertile or drought-stricken soils, or into urban slums. Then plantation monoculture and peasant misuse of crowded marginal lands (leading to deforestation, soil exhaustion, erosion, and so on), plus slum deterioration, lead to ecological and human devastation. Together with population increases, this process contributes to what I refer to as the worsening socioeconomic-environmental catastrophe, in which the poverty tends to be worse than the original poverty, the land and people have less potential for development to support the growing population, and the economy and society begin to collapse. (There is no need to take land and resources by force as long as the unwary peasants or their government will take printed money instead.[5])

The second reason is that, if any government money *is* created for poor people, international alarm about potential hyperinflation and currency depreciation quickly sets in. Many central banks in poor countries thus do not dare to create money for use by governments and the poor. In other words, either there is government action and hyperinflation or there is government inaction and mass unemployment— sometimes one after the other until the country becomes a "failed state" with no solution except perhaps through parallel commodity money. In other words, *(unbacked) bank-money creates poverty and dispossession.* Therefore we need to find other ways to preserve the institution of money creation without its risks, such as through the production and sale of a national gold-backed commodity money, parallel to and market-convertible into an existing "convertible" bank money in which international investors and governments have confidence.

Let us analyze the money institution abstractly. Trusted, convertible (into other convertible currencies) money—the only money willingly held because it maintains its value and convertibility (which was originally based on gold) because domestic and international investors and governments had confidence in it—may qualify to be called *international* convertible money. That is, it is the sum of bank monies created nationally by internationally trusted banks and by bank systems of trusted countries with convertible money. Such international convertible money is loaned primarily to internationally or nationally creditworthy customers in internationally trusted countries, and is owned primarily by the residents and corporations of the rich, trusted countries and by Third World elites.[6] If the poor peoples without trusted money try to interfere with this system, creating lack of bank confidence in their governments and currencies, international corporations can decamp and (try to) take their money capital with them, leaving the poor peoples and their countries with declining or worthless currencies, unworkable economies, and, of course, drastically worse poverty. There is nothing to back their currencies except confidence and convertibility (which they don't have) and desired exports (which they do have). They are told, "Be good, leave the system alone, and export rich resources, or you will be poor, with your money rendered worthless by the stroke of a pen"—and it is so.

Such is the nature of the international convertible money "confidence game." Indeed, even money created by trusted institutions is subject to the earlier limitations on its inflationary nature. Internationally trusted national banking systems create internationally trusted convertible national money ("as good as gold") out of nothing, in return for creditworthy borrowers' promises to repay money debts plus interest in the same money (or money that is convertible into it)—that is, the world money supply must expand. This internationally trusted convertible money is so trusted, desired, and depended on (provided inflation is avoided), that borrowers can buy up other nations' assets with it, as Canada's key assets are being bought up. Yet if others than internationally trusted banking systems try to create money, their money will not be trusted, convertible, or valuable.[7] Third World currencies thus frequently decline in value, leading to capital flight, collapsing exchange rates, runaway inflation, economic disasters, "failed state" economies, and poverty and suffering for all who depend on money—in other words, most of the world's population. *Confidence money is the worst cause of worldwide poverty*, and it is little understood. Do you, for example, understand the above system? Well, you aren't meant to. But you are meant to look up to and desire convertible currencies, thus increasing their value.

Indeed, if even trusted banking systems create increases in national monies faster than increases in the respective volumes of national output, national prices will start to rise and trusted monies will decline in value. And if the total of all trusted national money supplies (the total international convertible trusted money supply) rises faster than total world output rises—as it often does (cf world food and oil prices)—world prices will increase, at least for major internationally traded commodities and companies that produce resources and own land and real estate, and anything limited in supply relative to growing demand—and world money values will fall, at first steadily, then increasingly rapidly. The result: hyperinflation, until the world economy crashes or collapses, possibly with wars in between, and possibly before the effects of global warming take their toll.

The above process goes like this: Eventually holders of these trusted monies will start to ask what is backing their bank money IOUs that are losing value. The purchasing power of their incomes, savings, bonds, pensions, and so on is being lost, and they are becoming poorer—for example, many middle-class people cannot now afford to buy a house in our major cities. When such money holders experience lasting price increases, and when they realize that nothing except confidence-money debts and "convertible" IOUs are backing the confidence money created by trusted banks, they will start buying other, "real" assets that they believe will better store value and protect them from inflation. But when they do that, prices start rising faster, spending on inflation-hedge assets starts to accelerate, hyperinflation looms, and the whole world banking house of unbacked debt money threatens to come tumbling down.

We thus acquire what might be called an interest-rate or money-income-on-money standard of money value that rewards only banks and speculators, leaving most of the rest of us out in the cold and the billions of poor people desperate—the dispossessed cannot afford to buy land to get income from it or a home to reduce their costs. This standard or system is operated at the cost of people without money, debtors, and the poor people and debtor nations of the world. Such people and nations suffer from inflation by losing the value of their money capital and income, if any, and suffer from recession/depression by losing their income. Only the rich own "real" capital that helps them become rich from inflation while billions become poverty-stricken. Indeed, in a true monetary collapse, even the rich will lose their wealth and struggle to survive.

Thus one major reason for lasting poverty amongst the majority of the world's people is the world's bank-money system, with unbacked bank money created by the rich, for the rich, and to keep them rich, so that the rich and their dependants will support the world bank-money system (and the associated legal, police, property, and military systems) and keep the poor poor. Nothing other than reform of this system will tackle the poverty of nations. And reform involves governments manufacturing gold-backed commodity money to operate parallel to bank-created unbacked confidence money.

Commodity Money Introduced

When a country has a central bank that is able along with the private banks to create (unbacked) money and use it to trade for domestic goods and services and foreign exchange, that unbacked money, which has no intrinsic value, has its price(s) determined in domestic and foreign markets (supply and demand, convertibility) and by intangible confidence. It fluctuates and is not stable, and because of exponential money-supply increases (and other supply-and-demand forces such as population growth, resource exhaustion, and human behaviour, including war) tends to decline through inflation and devaluation. This tendency to decline means that it is not a good store of value for savings and eventually will lose (almost) all of its value, putting the monetary economy into crisis and eventual depression or hyperinflationary failure (except for owners of real property).

This conclusion suggests that something else with intrinsic value should be used for a back-up currency and savings role in case unbacked bank money loses value, although bank money should be preserved for the spending/circulating and related functions that it performs so well. One alternative for the savings role is parallel commodity money.

In my book *Canada Savings Coins* and my newsletter *The Economic Analyst*, I discussed the idea that a parallel commodity money system is needed, with the following findings. We cannot continue to depend on our unbacked bank-money system alone, because there is nothing to back it and stop it declining in value. In fact it has to and does constantly inflate and lose value, except when dangerous recession sets in. But we cannot do without bank money because all economic activity depends on it. Therefore, whatever action we take to produce and sell parallel commodity money units with intrinsic value must be in addition to or parallel to our present unbacked money system, not in place of it (unless it collapses). A parallel commodity money system in conjunction with the present unbacked bank money system is thus the most reasonable proposition.

What is proposed is the minting of a gold-containing coin by the government (through the national mint) that has a face or legal tender value greater than its gold-content value (when minted), as a savings vehicle and long-term back-up currency. This real-value (backed) money would be parallel to the present virtual or unbacked circulating bank money. It would not be added to present money-supply measurements because it serves a different (savings) purpose and would be impossibly inconvenient as circulating currency. It could be introduced into the money function of the economic system by being sold (with a rationing system) at government outlets for its initial face value. Say it contained 1/20 ounce ($40 to $50 worth) of gold at the start, with a face value of $100 and an even higher market value if the price of gold rose. This face value would be guaranteed by the government as convertible into $100 Canadian bank money in unbacked banknotes, if desired, and could be sold at a higher numerical value if the dollar value rose with the price of gold.[8]

There would be no threat to the unbacked bank-money system because the coins would (initially) be worth more in guaranteed bank money than in the market for gold, but savers buying these coins could rest assured that they would not be wiped out if inflation or depression got out of control. The government would make a profit, to be divided between minting/handling costs and government programs (for example, poverty-relief programs such as rural development), and additional employment benefits would come from the minting, distribution, and sales markup. (Incidentally, these coins would be "made by work and resources" and thus qualify as "goods" that could be added into the GNP and exported, adding to the positive balance of payments. They could thus be exported without exchange controls or balance-of-payments deficits. Bank money, on the other hand, which is only "currency," does not add to the GNP or the positive balance of payments, and thus might be subject to "capital flight" controls in a country with foreign-exchange problems. Note also that the coins could be worth more at home than abroad, except when they are sold at a premium, which would benefit the country.)

The problems mentioned earlier of exponential growth of the bank-money supply (money inflation) and prices (price inflation) are not solvable with an unbacked (debt) money system alone. They are also not solvable with a backed (by gold, for instance) money system alone. The first system leads eventually to exponentially accelerating inflation, devaluation, and hyperinflationary collapse; the second system, by not expanding rapidly, leads quickly to deflationary collapse. The two monetary systems must therefore run *in parallel* to keep the economy prosperous—though slightly inflationary—and to protect savings so that people feel more secure and are not so anxious to buy inflation-hedge assets, thus dangerously accelerating inflation.

A practical program could be planned as follows: Have the government pay the mint (with money borrowed from the banks!) to produce coins containing a small amount of gold (bought with borrowed money). The initial (government-created) face value would be higher than the gold-content value—for example, a face value of C$100 and a gold-content value of 1/20 ounce, or about C$40 to C$50—so that the government could finance the system and make a profit to use for purposes such as rural development. Citizens would thereby have an opportunity to buy an inflation hedge with a full-price buy-back guarantee of $100 per coin, an inflation hedge that is not also a cost-of-living item, but which keeps its value if inflation takes off.

Informal variants of the above system are in operation already. In nations with a weak currency needing exchange controls, people may prefer the U.S. dollar or the euro to the national or regional currency because of high and rising local prices or lack of confidence in the local currency. They therefore pay a premium price to obtain and save these relatively "hard," convertible, acceptable currencies, which they use for trips abroad, capital flight, or pensions. They also reserve this money for buying items that are sold only for hard currency, such as land and real estate, jewellery and gold, and imported luxury items. At the same time they are using local currency for everything else, in effect maintaining a dual or parallel currency system.

There is no doubt that money supplies are increasing, and have to increase, exponentially (see Figure 8). These increases are an important factor in price inflation as well. Eventually unbacked bank money will lose much of its value. People with money, sensing this already, are buying up "real" or inflation-hedge assets, pushing up their prices and accelerating inflation further, leaving the poor behind in poverty and bringing monetary collapse closer, perhaps with a couple of recessions in between. Most of us don't anticipate this yet, but when we do there will be a rush for the exits—out of local bank money and into . . . what? When that happens, the economy will stop dead. We can't do much to protect ourselves from such a development, except perhaps by becoming as self-sufficient as possible, and we can't prevent collapse by returning to the gold standard. But collectively we can bring some stability to the system by providing a gold-backed parallel currency that does not lose value—other crises aside—and that is convertible into and out of the depreciating bank debt money at a minimum or rising bank-money price.

In March 1998 and February 2000 I wrote to Mr. T. T. Mboweni, governor of the South African Reserve Bank, suggesting the minting of "value-added" gold coins—perhaps to be called Mandela rands—in South Africa, for reasons similar to those outlined above. In March 2000 I received a letter from his office that stated: "The Governor found your thoughts very interesting and commented that the idea of the Mandela Rand is receiving attention locally and may perhaps materialise some time in the future." An earlier letter, from the South African Department of Finance in May 1998, noted: "It is possible that the gold producers, the Rand Refinery or the South African Mint may elect to produce a 'four-nines' [pure gold] 1 oz gold coin with or without buy-back guarantees." (This correspondence is reproduced in Appendix B.) These encouraging comments made me feel that my theoretical work had neither been wasted nor found wanting at high practical levels—and I wanted my readers to know that.

CHAPTER 3

Demand and Distribution Theories

What Is Demand and What Is Supply?

Since this book talks about supply and demand, before considering economic ideologies it seems best to clarify what constitutes supply and what constitutes demand. As we'll see shortly, the distinction is not always clear, and sometimes a measure has both supply and demand characteristics. And the analysis also brings out some interesting points.

Let us start by considering subsidies, or per unit grants on things produced. If these subsidies are used to increase wages and profits by rewarding the producers and thereby encouraging more supply, and if demand is sufficient, then subsidies are supply incentives. If subsidies are used to reduce prices by helping consumers and thereby encouraging more demand, then subsidies are demand incentives. If subsidies are used to increase competitiveness by both increasing profits and reducing prices, then subsidies are both supply and demand incentives.

Now consider mercantilism, welfare, and balanced growth. If a supply business is in a poor area, it may not find (for example, by asking around) adequate local demand for its potential supply. But if local demand increases, perhaps through urban expansion or a new car assembly plant nearby, the potential supply may become actual new supply in response to the demand increase—a demand-creates-supply situation. So consider the case of a poor, isolated rural area with no economic attractions except the people who call it home. If a more generous state welfare program is introduced by a senior government, the benefits will be like increased "exports" (demand), bringing money into the area and creating additional local demands, such as for a local retirement home (which will earn supply dollars). Then demand will again have created supply (of retirement-home beds at a price) and the retirement home's services supply (earnings) will increase local demand for other things—the basic argument for "balanced growth" as a development plan for reducing poverty.

Marxism and Inadequate Demand

Demand-side theories, accordingly, are those that concentrate on money demand, particularly its adequacy, as *the* primary determinant of prosperity, job creation, and poverty reduction, and on inadequate demand as the main cause of recession/depression, unemployment, and poverty. These theories rule a large part of the world and of economic history, and therefore should be carefully understood in order to tackle poverty.

A capsule summary of Marxist theory can be rendered thus: private ownership of the means of production => labour theory of value => inequality and unspent surpluses => *inadequate demand* => depression, unemployment, immiserization, imperialism, war, and poverty. Marxist analysis is brilliant and powerful, considering where it started. It gives an original explanation of the poverty of billions; calls for revolution, expropriation, and dictatorship to remove the causes; and has resulted in both politico-military and ideological revolutions. In particular, Marx claimed that the classical economists were wrong in their claim that supply creates its own demand, and argued that inadequate demand was possible, present, and destructive. Almost a century later, Keynes agreed that inadequate demand was the essential cause of depressions and poverty, and he gave a better proof that inadequate demand was possible, present, and destructive.

The Marxist analysis was briefly as follows. The true value of commodities is the value of the labour embodied in them. But private owners of capital and land charge more than this labour value (otherwise they could not produce and employ) and receive "surpluses"—of interest, rent, and profits. Because of inequality and greater wealth than needed, these surpluses are not all spent on consumption. But as long as business is expanding, the surpluses can be spent on or reinvested in new productive capital, thus maintaining demand and employment as long as output is growing. Nevertheless, since the labour force cannot buy the whole expanding product at surplus-inflated prices, demand must eventually become inadequate, factories must close, workers must be laid off, and depression and "immiserization of the proletariat" must be the normal order of things under private ownership of the means of production. This would continue until, as Marx expressed it, the "workers of the world united and threw off the chains of capitalism," placing the means of production in the hands of the state (ruled by a "dictatorship of the proletariat"), which would spend any and all surpluses and keep people employed (even if unproductively and even if the state did not know how to run banks, businesses, farms, hospitals, utilities, and so on, despite its talk of "planning"). Before that time, the capitalist states, suffering depression, loss of markets, and loss of profits, plus unemployment and poverty, would seek new markets through mercantilism, imperialism, and war, threatening widespread death, destruction, and suffering in the search for profits (or mercantilist trade surpluses). Powerful stuff indeed, even if it does not provide a peaceful and permanent solution.

Marxism has divided the world and has generated anger and anti-capitalist sentiment in billions, though in the past decades it has become reduced in scope and less powerful—except in capitalist/communist China—and divided into different ideological groups. It has also diverted attention from what really makes economies work.[1] What it has succeeded in doing is to show some reasons why economies do *not* work (inequality, inadequate demand, mercantilism, imperialism, failed societies, dictatorship), that is, exploitation reasons for poverty. This opens the question "What is poverty?" to several additional answers, such as suffering from ideologies such as capitalism, communism, and mercantilism, and from population explosion, resource exhaustion, environmental destruction, and so on, which are not amenable to kindly charity and aid.

We have thus been handicapped by Marxism's violent criticism and lack of attention to the details of supply and how things work, and diverted from studying more effective remedies and how we can win support for them. But we have also been alerted to the poverty-causing evils of inequality, exploitation, and inadequate demand.[2] In our new-found single-minded emphasis on environmentalism, a possible danger is that we may overlook what this book is about, namely human poverty, its economic causes, and its difficult remedies. Nevertheless, we cannot ignore either the above communist analysis or the new environmentalist arguments, because to do so would make us ignorant of much of what makes the world go 'round.

Socialism and Redistribution

Whereas Marxism is analytical and leans towards the revolutionary, socialism is more philosophical and "distributional." In relation to poverty, this makes it harder to summarize socialism equally precisely, but the task is interesting and educational nevertheless. While partly dating back to early religious philosophies, socialism in its modern form began essentially as a product of the early nineteenth century. Lacking the strict analytical ideology of Marxism, it began as a protest against the misery of the factory system and as a means by which the exploited working class could defend itself against the hard new masters through organization: labour unions, political parties, cooperatives. It was an indictment of the capitalist system, which in addition to its inequities was unable to prevent recurrent wars and financial crises.

Socialism took up the idea that misery and injustice (poverty) were the result of the division of society into rich and poor. For the most part, socialist parties work within the framework of the capitalist state to secure, preferably by reform, the political power they require to shape both the institutions and the economic structure of society to their ends, for example, by heavy taxation of wealth and through trade unions and the welfare state. Thus they aim to achieve adequate demand and full employment without the expansionism of Keynes and the wealth incentives of both capitalism and Keynes.

After reform or revolution, some parties held that a dictatorship was necessary for the period of transition to socialist democracy or to the socially conscious capitalist democratic societies that many operate within now—which would provide full employment, free education and medical services, old-age pensions, unemployment insurance, and so on. Others, generally the more successful, chose a democratic route. The welfare state was declared to be the proper function of the state. Only later were the supply functions of expert (government) planning and administration of production and distribution mentioned in their messages.

But much was said about redistribution: progressive taxes, powerful trade unions, identifying and removing inequality and inadequate demand as the main causes of depression and poverty—like Marx and Keynes, by government borrowing and deficit spending and, after Keynes, by monetary expansion/creation, but not expropriation (except among extremists). As left-wing demand-siders, socialists have shifted the policy emphasis in many countries towards the welfare state.[3] This welfare state relieves poverty widely but is not a total solution as long as money/inflation and supply/production/incentive problems are not solved. And everyone, including the socialists, is now getting onto the environmental bandwagon, which was largely ignored before.

Keynesianism and Deficit Spending

The goal of Keynesianism was to restore adequate demand through government deficits (deficit spending) and low interest rates to encourage investment and consumption spending[4] with expanding money supplies. These tools, rather than Marxist expropriation or punitive socialist taxation, were to be used to tackle poverty and overcome unemployment and depression. It should be noted that Keynes agreed with Marx that inadequate demand was the chief cause of depression and poverty, and with the socialists that part of the solution could be found in the welfare state, but he defended private property and the capitalist system as the best means of running the economy. Note also that Keynes's system did not reform capitalism or the money and banking system but stored up more inflation, more debts, more balance-of-payments deficits, and more monetary instability. It also beat against the limits of environmental sustainability and led towards monetarism, supply-side economics, the New Right and the Common Sense Revolution, and monetary collapse.

Keynes did not really answer Marx. He answered the conventional theorists who argued that lasting depressions were impossible. Their arguments were that markets would reduce wages until everyone who wanted could find work, and reduce interest rates until savings fell and almost anyone with a good credit rating and a good investment project could borrow money to invest— that is, until saving was made equal to investment, so that saving (or non-spending) was returned to the income-spending stream through investment; naturally there would be neither inadequate demand nor depression. Keynes had to break down this barrier in order to advance.

What Keynes did was to show theoretically that there could indeed be lasting inadequate demand, mass unemployment, and depression. During the Great Depression there was such, and it was caused (circularly) by inadequate demand. This was because (1) if a downturn led to high unemployment and then wages were reduced, demand would fall further, creating continued inadequate demand, factory closures, worse unemployment, and depression; and (2) again, if there was inadequate demand for a while, and therefore very low profits, then even zero interest rates—assuming that lenders would risk lending money for no reward—would not lead employers to invest and take risks (with their own plus borrowed money) without adequate prospects of profit. In other words, employment and demand would not automatically recover and ensure a return to prosperity.

Then Keynes and his followers came up with their now-famous prescriptions for deficit spending, automatic stabilizers (of unemployment insurance and welfare spending) and low interest rates. The goal was to increase money supplies and spending and to preserve capitalism against the Marxist threat by maintaining or restoring adequate demand, profits, investment (to spend unspent savings), full employment and prosperity, and poverty relief. This is also powerful stuff, even if it leads eventually to higher expectations, more inflation, soaring government deficits and debts, and balance-of-payments difficulties, not to mention today's ecological stress and the dangers of hyperinflationary collapse and failed states. Keynesianism also represented right-wing opposition to socialist punitive taxation, even if it did not oppose the government deficit spending attacked by the monetarists.

Later on, Keynes's inflationary expansionism led to monetarism, supply-side economics, and anti-tax, New Right "common sense" revolutions, plus potential debt implosion in rich countries. In poor countries, supply may not respond so quickly to demand increases without rising prices, governments have more limited revenues and creditworthiness, and central banks may have less resistance to demands for more money, and less ability to protect the currency. In these countries Keynesian ideas lead rapidly to accelerating inflation, collapsing currencies, governments in trouble, and failed states (with their concomitant terrible poverty), or to rejection of the Keynesian prescriptions by *not* running deficits and creating money, and thus not remedying unemployment and poverty.

Keynesianism (or simple maladministration or expansion of the supply of unbacked confidence money) in poor countries means increasing inflation and poverty, mass un- or underemployment, domestic depression, weak business conditions, a discouraging investment climate, lack of development, capital flight, and worsening socioeconomic-environmental catastrophes or failed states. Ignorant, unwanted peasants ruin the hinterlands by stripping the forests and eroding the soil, then flock in unemployed mass poverty to the city slums at home and abroad, scaring away capital and the elites who might have employed them. Filled with dangerous anger, they invade the rich settlements and countries, bringing with them absolute, potentially violent poverty, and perhaps even terrorism and mass rebellion.

Keynesian economics and confidence money are thus not solutions for regions and nations that cannot create their own money and keep it reliable and trusted internationally. This may seem a rather drastic statement from a Western-trained economist. What can I possibly offer after denying what I have learned? I hope the answer lies in this book, in which I have carefully analyzed the major economic and monetary systems, pointed out where they fall down, and offered my own remedies, without malice,[5] (including parallel commodity money and rural development).

Monetarism

Marxism was, and socialism more mildly is, a reaction to inequality and inadequate demand causing poverty. Keynesianism has been a reaction to depression and inadequate demand causing poverty. And recent monetarism, supply-side theories, and New Right politics are reactions to Keynesian expansionism and welfarism, alleging that inflation, high taxes, welfare dependency, and resulting inadequate *supply* are causes of poverty. It is a problem and a tragedy that, with everybody in agreement that we must tackle poverty, we all seem ready to go to war, or at least to fight politically over how.

One difficulty with Keynesian deficit spending, welfare spending, and money expansion is that the combination of these three tends to increase demand too much, or more than supply. This leads to shortages and rising prices (or growing imports and a falling dollar) or to price and money inflation, which makes people with fixed incomes—or those who have been competed out of work by cheaper foreign products—poor, despite Keynesian intentions to overcome depression and poverty.

Monetarism (also known as the Austrian School or Friedmanism) says that inflation is due *only* to over-rapid increases in the money supply. We can disagree with this contention, saying, for example, that overspending (as in Keynesianism, socialism, and Marxism), wars, natural disasters, or rising environmental costs can increase demand-spending more than supply, or increase costs, causing prices to rise. But we can agree over inflation's harmful effects.

Accordingly, anti-inflation supply-side theories and New Right politics, such as Mike Harris's Common Sense Revolution, eventually come along and say that

- tax revenues, incentives, investments, and output growth are reduced when you raise tax rates too high, so income or all taxes should be cut;
- supply is increased by getting government off people's backs and reducing taxes and government spending;
- deficits and debts are bankrupting us and must be cut;
- therefore, all these excesses are causing inflation and unemployment;
- therefore, government spending, including welfare spending, must be cut drastically.

Mike Harris's Conservatives got elected in Ontario with a majority, despite reducing their care for the poor, because they promised a "common sense revolution." It collided with the "revolution of rising expectations," denying the Keynesian "revolution" and threatening a social uprising against overgenerous welfare programs and resulting rising unemployment, inflation, and poverty. A political reaction indeed—but sometimes it cuts deep, and that makes you think.

With a judicious selection of export, or at least output, promotion; adequate demand; the welfare state; progressive but not too high taxes, moderately stimulative monetary and fiscal policies; *and* parallel commodity money, we can go about as far as theory will take us. Specific measures such as monetary reform, land reform, and rural and regional development policies can cover most of the distance towards poverty alleviation on the theoretical or planning side. Then comes the translation into practice—yet another world—which I tried to approach with my analyses of mercantilism and reverse mercantilism, the L0L1P0 experiment, rural planning, and monetary reforms based on analysis of observation.

Just work this out along with me: We have to get sustainable production going (supply). Then we have to get it sold (demand), with just the right amount of money distributed and not too much inflation or unemployment, which lead to poverty or inequality. And we have to do this without monetary breakdown, consistently, without population explosion, war, or environmental destruction. Each is only one step, but all are essential. Balanced learning and peace thus become the *sine qua non*s of life.

CHAPTER 4

Agricultural, Rural, and Regional Development

To round off this mercantile, monetary, political/ideological and rural/urban/ environmental analysis of the poverty of nations, we can start by looking down at the earth from above. When we do this, we can see the vastness and complexity of the lands from which different peoples extract their food and resources, often leaving behind deserts and very frequently living a life of poverty. The dwellers on these lands, most of whom have little money and limited resources, bear a heavy workload on gradually (or rapidly) depleting soils. Population explosion is causing them to exceed the carrying capacity of their lands, forcing migratory escape to the cities. The cities, in turn, even though they have performed miracles of economic growth, are becoming terribly overcrowded and poverty-stricken themselves, especially in poor areas on the fringes, and particularly in depressed economic times. One cause of urban poverty is partly this constant, massive influx from rural areas and partly faults in bank-money systems, leading to inflation, anti-inflation policies, recession, unemployment, inequality and more poverty. Such "ecological migration" and monetary instability are threatening to become major world poverty problems, along with pollution/ global warming and soil erosion.

Poverty is a widespread result of the above causes, but the vicious circle seems to start with the land. So let us complete the recommended quadruple solution—reverse mercantilism, parallel commodity money, ideological reform, and agricultural/ rural/ regional development—by seeking to improve the rural areas.

The Environment and Human Ecology

Economics and environmentalism should work together, not fight each other. Otherwise there will not be the jobs and money needed to get the environmental work done, nor a liveable planet on which to enjoy the fruits of our labour. In this section I will try to put both fields into a constructive joint perspective.

The poverty problem may be viewed as a human ecology problem if we attribute human weaknesses to failure in humanity's ecological and survival adaptations—for example, in human/political relations, in war, and in the institutions of money and banking, as well as in land allocation, resource destruction, and so forth. Mercantilism, imperialism, and capitalism set nations against one another, and Marxism and other ideologies try to break others' systems down; each set of beliefs is a cause of massive poverty and war. This study of poverty thus finds enough material in the economic sphere to keep one's mind busy, leaving ecological scholarship to others even while remaining acutely aware of how intertwined these two disciplines should be.

Economic theories and ideologies often, as with Adam Smith's, begin with poverty, and sometimes with ecological degradation (as in Jared Diamond's *Collapse*). They seek prosperity through productivity improvement, trade gains, income and wealth redistribution, monetary manipulation, exploitation of people and environments, and political, economic, monetary, and environmental reforms. Now that "development" has gone so far, economic systems could finish with ecological destruction—and have already done so in some instances. Therefore poverty remedies should tread a fine line between developing in traditional exploitative ways and caring for the environment as well, using lessons drawn from ecology. That is to say, conservation, sustainability, ecological sensitivity, and so on should be practised in development, but development of the right economic kind is also needed to tackle poverty without harmful side effects.

Not only is infinite development impossible in a finite world, but finite development of the wrong kind can cause poverty, environmental destruction, human disaster, and potentially worse poverty to come. These very real problems already exist widely and combine to produce the (worsening) socioeconomic-environmental (and political) disaster, or "failed state," scenarios that arise from phenomena such as the following:

- exploding populations exceeding the carrying capacities of their lands, destroying the peace and/or the environment, and then taking their problems elsewhere
- international corporations and plantations temporarily sustaining these exploding populations in reserved areas, but concentrating the non-elites first in marginal rural areas and second in city shanty-slums, leading to excessive urbanization and dependent insecurity. They remain always ready to move their capital elsewhere if land and other resources become exhausted or if the market or political outlook becomes unpromising, thus threatening to leave mass "surplus" populations to fester in abject poverty and to seek emigration to rich countries' cities.
- ecologically harmful technologies such as corporate resource exhaustion and monoculture, pollution of many kinds, and peasant land devastation, destroying the land and the total national carrying capacity. This leads to social, economic, and environmental collapse ("The soil cannot keep them any more") and to mass rural unemployment, poverty, and emigration—even partly,

during depressions, in developed countries—plus diseases such as AIDS plus crime, corruption, unrest, terrorism, and so on.

- simple trade and monetary breakdowns causing collapses.

The marginalized people from less developed (often exhausted and partly destroyed) hinterlands transport their poverty to, and intensify it in, polluted, heavily unemployed, socially devastated, unequal cities at home and abroad, and they threaten political as well as socioeconomic and environmental crises in their new homes as well as their old. The resulting crises threaten the corporations, capital, and elites that might employ the poor, engendering capital flight and elite emigration. Thus the poor are threatened with being left not only to starve and suffer in unemployed poverty, but also to have no solution and no hope beyond crime and terrorism. This problem is so great that out-migration is likely to be a major issue in the future. As argued earlier, the poor peoples may be unable to do anything about this unless they copy their former exploiters through reverse mercantilism in order to regain wealth, or through non-destructive socialism and cooperative entrepreneurship to create and redistribute wealth without harming supply—and through following the lessons of this book, such as monetary reform (parallel commodity money) and land reform leading to agricultural, rural, and regional development.

This book began with despair over a non-productive hinterland, moved on to suggest reverse mercantilism to bring money back to such hinterlands, found that the sought-out oases were overcrowded and unemployed, and tackled that problem with a theory of parallel commodity money. Assuming that the recommended theory was put into successful practice, I argued that the cities and/or governments so assisted should then help develop the devastated hinterlands from which so many of their inhabitants had come, as a rounded theoretical solution to rural and urban poverty in many parts of the world.

Development of the Approach

At the beginning of this odyssey into poverty alleviation, I found it impossible to do much from the rural side of affairs, largely because of a lack of investment money and enough capable people to get rural development going, and sometimes because of a lack of secure land titles to encourage investment or even satisfactory infrastructure. The best people were often leaving the land to seek their fortune in the cities.

Then I discovered that not all workers were leaving the land permanently; many were only migrating temporarily to bring money back home (mainly for consumption rather than productive investment purposes). I coined the term *reverse mercantilism* to describe this temporary flow of people out to earn money and the money earned flowing back in. This phase could not satisfactorily be permanent because it consists of temporary migrants overcrowding the already packed city slums, aggravating the already high unemployment rate, and for the time being reducing output in the abandoned rural areas and average income in the overcrowded urban areas. So the solution had to include increased employment in the urban areas to increase income and living capacity there, and to raise remittances to the rural areas to ease poverty and spark development there.

The increased-employment route was blocked by the monetary phenomenon of stimulative unbacked money leading to inflation, and the fear of inflation leading to inadequate stimulus. So I devised the mechanism of dual or parallel currencies: one a gold-backed, non-inflationary currency for inflation-hedge savings and for reducing inflation of other inflation-hedge assets, and the other the freer, non-inflation-hedged bank money to increase employment without destroying people's savings. This was the parallel commodity money argument, designed to improve economic conditions in both urban and rural areas. On a different tack, distributional reform may be an important, large-scale remedy. That left the only policy plan lacking: agricultural, rural, and regional development to reduce the rural-urban influx by improving conditions in the rural areas as well.

This last of the quartet of economic measures needed depends on investments made in each of three phases. These investments are (1) migrant labour in the first phase, (2) "real" monetary expansion in the second, and (3) land profits and taxes in the third. In the first phase, migrant labourers could be legally granted private property titles on credit to land owned by tribal chiefs or the government. These properties would create "instant capital" that would appreciate during the second two phases and could be used as backing for loan-capital investments to assist development during the third. The seigniorage and profits from the government-created parallel coinage could be allocated to this agricultural, rural, and regional development scheme. The development expenses and capital required for the key—and delightful!—third phase could come from the other two phases: from taxes on income and land and the profits created thereby, and from liquidation of created land capital. All the above would then make possible an expanding development program such as those described in the development literature and below, but this time with its own domestic private capital!

All this requires planning on an enormous scale, preferably using the tools of the market economy, but recognizing that many great problems are social in nature (for instance, several great cities are already becoming congested, uneconomic, lethally polluted, and otherwise dangerous to life). Planning needs to go beyond the above generalities about reverse mercantilism, parallel commodity money, distributional reform and the need for environmentally conscious land development. However, these beginnings are a useful start in that they employ the monetary mechanism to spread the money around, to keep it sufficient and honest (that is, valuable), and then to point out that investment must eventually flow out of the cities into the rural areas. That is a valuable beginning, without even considering planning.

Underlying the above quartet of economic ideas is one simple sentence: *Development (i.e., poverty alleviation) is a matter of getting money circulating everywhere.* Wherever money is, there people tend to go—to "get money," as Adam Smith said. Try it: almost everything that has been said in this book, and in many others, can be summed up in this sentence.[1] Carrying on with this theme, we find that poverty alleviation under conditions of rural insufficiency (lack of money and the means of getting money) requires a carefully balanced and financed program involving such elements as the following:

- *money*: a minimum income for everyone, carefully structured, so that dire poverty is alleviated and people spend where and on what they need, without destroying work incentives, developing local distributors and producers (and jobs!); also, subsidies to encourage agricultural production (see

Appendix C, on the coupon system used in Malawi) and soil conservation;

- *jobs*, such as those found by migrant workers in the cities, then those developed in the rural areas;
- *land reform and land titles*, so that as many people as possible acquire a means to earn money (supplemental if necessary), and an encouragement to care for the land;
- *basic infrastructure planning*, spreading out from present facilities;
- *economic development* activities and personnel to promote production and soil conservation—for example, agricultural demonstration and training/teaching stations (see below), agricultural extension and other technically skilled workers, experienced leading farmers, and businessmen-investors;
- *human and social development* workers such as teachers, health-care staff, social workers, and community development facilitators (in "growth points"), as well as community leaders, professionals (lawyers, accountants), and religious leaders.

Land Reform, Land Development, and Agricultural Teaching Stations

One of the major obstacles to rural development that aims to keep more people in the rural areas may be inequality in land ownership. This is a very delicate issue. Expropriation, as in Zimbabwe, may lead to agricultural and economic collapse. No action may mean working with too little land and money and too many people, an impossibility that faced me at the beginning of my odyssey. Accordingly, means should be found to grant title to small non-land-owning farmers while preserving some productive large farms, with changes, and to intensively develop them as illustrated in the diagrams below. Purchases could be made by a senior government agency using borrowed bank money. It could then subdivide the land into viable small farm lots (as in the L0L1P0 experiment) and hire a developer to install infrastructures: roads, water, electricity, sewers, possibly soil and water conservation facilities. Then the developed small farm lots could be sold on credit to eager new farmers for more than the purchase and development cost. The farmers would borrow from the same banks (against their new equity in their plots) to pay off the government agency, and the government initial-credit-granting agency would supervise the use of further credit and initial farming operations to ensure that the small farms became productive enough to pay off their loans and develop a successful economic "station." Wealthy private farmers, financiers, and developers (with appropriate skilled staff) could also perform this service in order to prevent collapse or stalemate.

Various designs can be drawn up (see Figures 10 to 11) to illustrate different types of government demonstration and teaching farms. These might be divided into small farm lots with cooperative or joint features (for example, teaching, processing, marketing), and possibly including stores and service centres. These nodes could possibly grow into villages—natural production-based agricultural, rural, and regional development "growth points"—which would help achieve the goal of "balanced" (rural/urban, agricultural/non-agricultural) development, leading to less poverty and crowding in both rural and urban areas.[2]

But what are we to do about this great problem from a rural standpoint? Speaking very carefully, because I don't want to undermine what is said above against monetary inflation, I would like to suggest that part of what is needed is being provided by food inflation! This "subsidy" will get money out to where it is needed for rural development, poverty alleviation and fighting the rural-urban crush. The next task would be to collect some of that new wealth for rural investments: physical infrastructures, development planning, soil conservation, agricultural and other education, etc. A subset of the latter would be farm and agricultural station development, as a basis for rural supply, exports, employment and re-population creation, as described in the text. even creative government and industrial expansion could bring money, jobs and entrepreneurs into the rural areas, and fill out the process of rural-development-to-relieve-urban-congestion so urgently needed.

Such stations, perhaps developed with parallel coin seigniorage profits, could make capital go further in terms of production and practical teaching than almost any other plan one might imagine. The development facilities can be put in; the land ploughed, terraced, and divided into lots; diverse crops chosen to deliver to a central processing and selling facility; and the duties and rights (including remuneration[3]) of the labourers/students/future farmers worked out. One possible approach is to allow each student-farmer a small homestead on which he or she could try to become as self-sufficient as possible—thus increasing rural output without having to deal with the problem of marketing—while selling/exporting through wage work on other land for the large station (total self-sufficiency being impossible). As a sideline, a well laid-out, fertile, irrigated, multiple-enterprise demonstration and teaching station could become a valuable tourist attraction. It would be like an enormous practical botanical garden, with walking and driving tours, information exhibits on each enterprise, a salesroom, a restaurant, even a hotel, much like the popular wineries of the Niagara region and British Columbia's Okanogan district.

Education and training are controversial means of promoting agricultural and rural development because they also promote rural-urban migration, urban overcrowding, and unemployment. If the rate of migration to the cities is not stemmed, city life—including jobs, housing, services, and general well-being—will not keep pace with the surge in population, and more education will lead to more migration and unemployment. But since education is necessary, it should be reformed, perhaps along the lines of the training proposed for the stations above, or at least with teachers so trained.

But this is not to forget the stations' principal role as aids to agricultural and rural development. Every region grows through

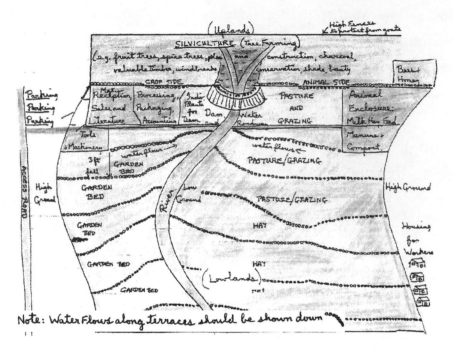

Figure 10: A government experimental demonstration land-reform settlement (terraced at 3 feet vertical spacing and 5% slope to river). This is an experiment to see what grows and how much it yields under simple technology with (supervised) peasant workers. It is meant to demonstrate and train so that other settlements can succeed, with these or other workers. Part of the idea is to record sales per each square foot so as to see how big a lot is required to be viable, with and without irrigation. Workers would receive minimum wage plus a share of the profits. The government would provide funding and charge rents.

export promotion and import substitution (plus self-sufficient output), and these activities, along with processing and marketing, are precisely what the stations are designed to develop (plus jobs, housing, villages, and so on). The word *village* brings us back to the sensitive core of the subject: rural depopulation and urban overcrowding. The stations are corrective steps; they are meant to increase rural population and output and bring money into the rural regions, teaching practical agriculture and in the process creating both on- and off-farm jobs, even villages with stores, service stations, restaurants, and so on. Villages then tend to create

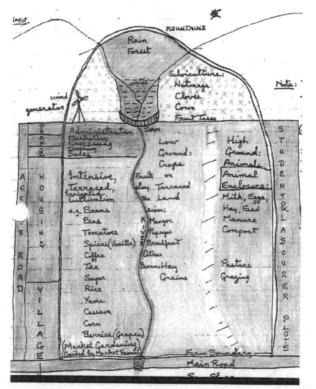

Figure 11: A government or university agricultural development and teaching station.

their own jobs, attracting people back from urban unemployment and all the other disadvantages of city life. We could begin to escape from the world of Alan Paton's sad lament "The soil cannot keep them anymore."

This task is never-ending. It is very difficult to achieve successful rural development through agricultural improvement alone. In my own region of Simcoe County, "agriculture declined from first to last among the major economic sectors between 1951 and 1991, despite good land, location, roads, utilities, and technology, subsidies, education and extension services and adequate water."[4] The L0L1P0 small-farm experiment showed that considerable intensification is not only possible but necessary for successful farming in a crowded rural area. Complete self-sufficiency is impossible; off-farm or "export" sales are necessary, and the latter may require the cooperation of a larger group.

Urban people in poor countries may not want to go back to the fields, mostly because small-scale agriculture might not give them the income needed for clothes, education, cellphones, television, and the myriad goods that are part of poor countries' new culture. It may be that city-dwellers couldn't do much with just bare "fields." However, I have proved that much can be achieved in the way of adequate income from adequate facilities with my small farm, which demonstrated that unemployed urban people are much worse off than productive small farmers. Small farmers can be prosperous, and land reform can work if it is done well.

My work in this area has not discussed cultural and political matters. I have focused on multi-plot stations, supervised by a foreman, with semi-independent plots and joint infrastructure and heavy equipment, that are designed to train non-farmers until they can make an independent (or cooperative) go of it on the land, aided by nearby transportation and villages. My paper "Creating Extra Values Out of Nothing" makes a straightforward argument:

> One method of tackling several of the problems (faced by poor and/or inexperienced farmers) at one time, is to have government borrow money to buy land, or use profits from the parallel coinage scheme to buy land; then "develop" this land (into small farms) as in an urban subdivision (with larger plots). Then equipped plots can be allocated under varying tenancies and purposes: e.g., plots can be owned by the landlord, such as an Agricultural College, which also employs and teaches the workers; or plots can be rented by learning farmers, who work and learn for their rent and small pay; or plots can be rental-purchased by future farm-owners-to-stay, who will work-learn now but eventually buy their farms at a profit to the College, "creating extra (capital) values out of nothing except labour," as in the gold coin example. The peasant-farmers of any land reform grouping would be trained as agriculturalists, while earning their keep and helping

produce-(and market)-to-pay the capital costs of the College (Government)-owned Station.[5]

I designed a similar government or university agricultural teaching station, meant to be run as a profitable enterprise while teaching student-farmer-workers who did not have their own plots. Students were to be taught intensified production, harvesting, processing, storage, marketing, and bookkeeping, and its role as a tourist attraction was to be emphasized. Theory was to be used to teach the economic benefits of export promotion (bringing money into the local area, where it can circulate), import substitution (keeping money, and jobs, in the rural area), and self-sufficiency (heavily protected products for one's own use that one does not have to sell—or buy!). Similar advantages come from local wind-generated or solar electricity and from processing products locally. Rural depopulation and urban overcrowding have blighted many developing countries; the stations could be corrective steps in the right direction.

The economic activities generated by the stations (plus those generated by utilities and new farmers) could eventually spin off whole villages with most of the facilities, services, and products that more urban environments can offer: stores, restaurants, garages, motels, churches, clinics, schools, bars, golf courses, playing fields, retirement homes, farmers' markets, newspapers, hairdressers, mechanics, road and utility maintenance, house construction and maintenance, and so on. Villages would thus create more jobs and markets, attracting people back from the overcrowded cities. For further development, governments could copy the South African program of decentralization by encouraging new investors through tax relief and other benefits to set up shop in country towns.

Preliminary Conclusions

To promote rural (supply) development in order to produce exports that will bring money into the rural areas, as recommended by Adam Smith and the mercantilists, we can use two complementary approaches. The first is to pick favoured locations for intensive or extensive development as individual farms (the LOLIPO approach) or as sites for large agricultural teaching and export stations (the mapped approach). The second is to attempt development planning as for a small country. Some details of the first approach are given above; further details of the second approach are summarized as follows.

1. Negotiate funds from a senior government for a development plan that includes
2. basic infrastructures, for example, roads, water, and electricity, starting from existing settlements, and
3. credit for one or more large "land reform" demonstration, teaching, and export agricultural estates, with small supervised plots, to get productive and export agriculture started and to stimulate development of new rural villages or growth points.
4. Obtain financing for the above investments from funds raised by producing parallel commodity money and

5. subsidies for agricultural and non-agricultural rural enterprises, for example, in processing and exporting agricultural products, building tourist resorts, retirement villages, clinics, light industries, and so on.

6. Then seek replication of urban and large industry development processes by domestic "colonization" of rural areas and regional redistribution of incomes and activities toward rural areas,

7. soil and water conservation facilities, and

8. facilities such as housing, schools, hospitals, and jails, and

9. resorts and other tourism facilities for such activities as golfing, swimming, conventions, and trade shows.

In ways such as these, promote balanced development of rural as well as urban areas, spread the monetary development of a commodity-based economy, and promote a non-inflationary approach to poverty alleviation.

My experience of agricultural and rural development has taught me that the simple and obvious things are rarely recognized. The most simple and obvious fact is that farmers (or group farming projects) have to combine realistic, practical planning with enough money, other resources, skills, and hard work to produce and process farm products for an accessible market at a profit—quite a job! Those concerned with rural communities must also develop their areas with other-than-agricultural services: infrastructure, especially transportation, electricity, and water; tourism; light industry; natural resource development; housing; facilities such as clinics, stores, banks, schools, and churches; and with non-agricultural labour, including commuting. These services may depend in turn on non-agricultural development of rural villages or even on this book's concept of a parallel commodity money to help provide markets for developing agricultural and non-agricultural rural industries.

Complementary government agricultural development, teaching, and land reform colleges could teach theory and practice, add processing, and attract tourism and village growth to increase development. All the above together show strong potential to promote agricultural and rural development. Then, with all four economic development policies in place, there should be room for future reforms such as soil and water conservation, other social and health improvements, and large-scale eradication of poverty—which, of course, is what we are aiming for.

CHAPTER 5

Findings and Conclusions

The main theses of this book are that (1) exploitation and lack of means of production necessitate reverse mercantilism for poor areas in dire straits; (2) the resulting lack of capital for jobs in the overcrowded recipient cities necessitates a parallel, gold-backed currency; (3) the accompanying inequality and unemployment necessitate resolution of ideological conflict (inequality reduction) to promote peace and prosperity; and (4) the accompanying rural-urban migration necessitates agricultural, rural, and regional development aided by the central government. All these stem from Adam Smith's insight "The great affair, we always find, is to get money" and the realization that political institutions, ideologies, monetary mechanisms, distribution theories, and regional development schemes are all about finding adequate demand, with a sideline on adequate supply—to get money (and goods) circulating everywhere.

Mercantilism today says, "Trade, not aid." Historically it meant trade surpluses to bring money into the country to stimulate domestic industry by overcoming inadequate demand, through getting adequate money into the hands of consumers. This export promotion and import substitution thesis applies, for example, to the country of Canada, the province of Ontario, the region of Simcoe County, and even units as small as a household or the L0L1P0 farm. It also applies to the tariff and trade policies of all countries. It applies, moreover, to the competitive production needs of all economic units and regions. However, poverty can be due not only to failures in production and trade but also to market and distribution failures, or inadequate demand, the core concern of the great economic-political schools such as capitalism, communism, socialism, Keynesianism, monetarism, and of course mercantilism. Poverty may also be due to lack of supply, requiring rural development. Accordingly, to remedy poverty we need to remedy the production and environmental systems, the trade system, the monetary system, the distribution system, and the unbalanced rural-urban system.

This book is about tackling poverty caused by mercantilism, monetary failings, unequal distribution of property and income, production failures, rural and ecological decline, and mistaken policies. It seeks to find remedies for these standing causes rather than for sudden crises and/or for individual relief; the latter problems are beyond the scope of one writer and require multiple skills, disciplines, and dollars to remedy. For example, who can help the victims of wars or natural disasters except sovereign states or organizations with practical skills such as Médecins sans frontières?

But collectively, with the right ideas, we can manipulate money and policies to create incomes and jobs, and maybe we can start on the environment. These latter solutions are what this book is about.

To give them more realism and practical value, my arguments are based on observation and experience as well as on book-learning and theorizing. For example, early observation and experience of a South African native reserve in the 1950s suggested that the poverty problem there was partly an agricultural problem. However, later studies showed that the main problem was apartheid, which made the reserves inadequate to support the exploding population and forced the Africans to use migrant labour, or "reverse mercantilism"—migrating temporarily to earn outside money instead of trying to sell export goods to bring money back in—in order to survive. Further observation and evidence showed that the same picture held for the poor West Indian islands, and indeed for massive immigration from around the world to the relatively rich countries and cities.

But reverse mercantilism causes overcrowding, unemployment, and other problems in the wealthy cities, and the "confidence money" system creates inflation and very high unemployment. Therefore remedial analysis suggests the introduction of parallel, gold-backed "commodity money" to help create jobs without runaway inflation. However, while reverse mercantilism and parallel commodity money might help reduce poverty and unemployment separately in poor rural and rich urban areas, these partial measures leave the rural-urban influx and resulting urban unemployment problems unsolved. This failure requires the introduction of a third complementary strategy, namely agricultural, rural, and regional development, to reduce flight from the land and to achieve a balanced-growth solution to both rural and urban poverty. A fourth complementary strategy is policies designed to redistribute unequal incomes and wealth.

Adam Smith gave us the statement "The great affair, we always find, is to get money," to which I add "or the means of getting money." This is reflected in the costs of getting the means and the reluctance to give them up, even though we often give up the products, not the money, capital, or land. It is also reflected in the poor countries' cry of "Trade, not aid" and in the rich countries' trade barriers "to keep jobs at home." Importantly, financial centres—which produce money that makes money to get money exponentially, at almost no cost and with almost no limits—get so large and so rich and expensive that the money-means of making money starts to break down, and they move towards collapse like the civilizations before them. We may be seeing the beginnings of this now: market records both high and low are showing the instability of money created out of nothing and with nothing to back it. Such a collapse could be the worst cause of worldwide poverty imaginable, and it must be prevented—for example, by parallel, gold-backed commodity money.

Meanwhile, the Canadian and Ontario governments exhibit pure mercantilism in their policies of export promotion and import substitution. Simcoe County in Ontario has grown entirely by export promotion and import substitution to get outside money and to keep it briefly circulating locally—mercantilistically—at home. My L0L1P0 small-farm experiment showed that no economic unit, small, medium or large, that does not earn its own convertible money by competitive supply/export expansion can achieve development and poverty alleviation. You cannot print yourself to riches or depend on aid, but have to get down to work to produce and export or sell, using means of earning money income. If you have no means and cannot produce and sell competitively, then you will remain poor and dependent on costly aid or welfare systems. My descriptions of the small-farm experiment and agricultural, rural, and regional development are intended to help tackle this "supply side" problem.

However, when a poor nation's supply/export escape is blocked by industrial nations' protectionism, the latter becomes a major cause of poverty, the only escapes from which are reverse mercantilism—export of people or labour—and/or tariff reform/reduction by developed nations. Even the alternative of self-sufficiency with a weaker currency is impossible if the region or nation does not control its money supply and value, or if the central bank blocks devaluation to hide inflation that would reflect on the competitive value of its currency.

The L0L1P0 small-farm experiment illustrates some of the practical steps that have to be taken to alleviate poverty by increasing production/supply and sales/created demand, and not attempting to develop by increasing monetary demand alone. Adequate demand to alleviate poverty applies only where production facilities are in place (it is much more difficult to create adequate supply facilities). A local farm—after developing production of a variety of products for roadside sale, as did the L0L1P0 experiment—opened up a village store on the highway and arranged a number of wider sales contracts to expand both supply and demand and to increase local jobs and incomes from the same land: a form of intensification.

When a new exporting enterprise is established that brings into a region the lifeblood of outside money, it multiplies local jobs and incomes, assists village expansion, acts as a spark for rural and regional development, keeps more people in the rural area, reduces the problem of rural-urban migration, and alleviates poverty all around. These achievements would be impossibly expensive for financial assistance alone; if you tried to achieve the same benefits through monetary handouts, all you would accomplish would be a collection of poor beggars—forever. This has to be borne in mind when considering my later advocacy of a minimum survival income for all, which would immediately reduce poverty on a large scale and might help increase local markets. It would have to be kept lower than, or supplemental to, minimum low-wage working incomes, so as not to create inflation and a larger dependent welfare class.

But if rural-urban migration cannot be reduced and urban unemployment keeps rising partly because of restrictive anti-inflation monetary policies, then unemployment poverty can be kept down only by introducing parallel, gold-backed commodity money to keep inflation low and allow monetary stimulus and employment expansion by stimulative policies without runaway inflation. These stimulative policies are what the monetary economy depends on to achieve growth and recovery from recession (with the help of capitalists!).

When there is "excess" income, as in the oil- and gas-producing region of Alberta and in some oil-exporting countries, the problem is not so much overall poverty as regionally unequal incomes and taxes, which push people out of work in the unfavoured regions or industries, partly by raising national (or regional) wages and currency values to uncompetitive levels. Perhaps the only equitable policies are regional redistribution of investment and/or a "heritage fund" such as that established in Alberta. Monetary policy should be expansionary—with relatively low interest rates—to keep exchange rates down, but fiscal policy should be restrictive—with high, progressive income taxes—to keep inflation down. Both of these approaches are opposed by the present powers that be, so a solution to unequal prosperity is not in sight. However, recession and lack of inflation are currently changing policies. The situation of unequal prosperity in Trinidad and Tobago provides an illustrative warning.

Chapter 1 said that South Africa was (and is) a mercantile creation, with areas of great wealth amid pockets of poverty. The desperately poor reserves were and are insufficient to support the Africans on the land. So the Africans crowded in to work in the "white" cities. But poverty was endemic in both reserves and cities, as detailed by Wilson and Ramphele in *Uprooting Poverty: The South African Challenge*. This poverty was hard to eliminate because the reserves were too small and the cities could not expand fast enough, partly because of the need for restrictive monetary policies to fight inflation. Therefore there were two initial requirements: one was reverse mercantilism, or exporting labour services to bring money back into the reserves, and the other was parallel commodity money, to enable the cities to absorb more labourers without runaway inflation. Later on, when funds become available, there will also be a need to "develop" the rural areas in order to stem the tide of the rural-urban influx.

Humanitarian but Practical Ideologies

I was so keen to discuss needed practical measures—reverse mercantilism, parallel commodity money, and rural development— that I almost forgot to write about a guiding ideology, partly because it is so controversial a subject. Tackling poverty implies a concern for the poor. Being an economist implies a concern for measures that work or are efficient. Being a fascinated traveller, student, and observer helps one begin.

There are so many poor people, needing and wanting so much, that it is impossible to care for all by means of aid alone. Yet mass poverty and inequality are so tragic and so dangerous that something great must be done. Therefore we need to help, not only by redistribution but also by helping the poor help themselves. And the poor are already helping themselves—in part, by crowding into places where the money is—but this rural-urban influx is causing so many problems that we must try to alleviate it. Needed measures include parallel commodity money and rural development, the latter requiring land reform by government and redistribution (by purchase) of large landholdings, as well as a very small and careful redistribution of money to the places where people now live, financed by a moderate redistribution of income plus production incentives of many kinds, for both rich and poor.

As to which ideological school this represents, I would say, "peacefully and wisely, all"—getting money, jobs, and the means of production, especially land, to all people in order to produce and consume what is needed. That is what I would call "loving thy neighbour as thyself."

In the "native reserves" lives were bleak. The overcrowded, eroded, third-rate land, abandoned by much of the labour force, produced almost nothing. Therefore the people left the land and migrated, supposedly temporarily, to the cities to earn some "outside" money to send back and support those still in the reserves. Thus their answer was reverse mercantilism, under which poverty—caused by mercantilism from the outside capturing the lands and resources of a subject people—was answered by reverse mercantilism from the inside: export of the remaining resource, labour, for survival, (to bring money back in).

Some examples of reverse mercantilism can be seen in Canada today. My wife, who comes from Fort Frances in northwest Ontario, remarked that the Native people used to be better off in Fort Frances than in Kenora, a neighbouring town. This was because many aboriginals lived right in Fort Frances and many more came in from the surrounding reserve to work in the paper mill. There was also intermarriage between Natives and whites, which was not often the case in and around Kenora. Reverse mercantilism can thus operate in any area where the conditions are right.

The pictures in this book illustrate in more detail the hinterland poverty that can lead to the uncomfortable extreme of reverse mercantilism: having to walk long distances every day to get water and firewood, to traverse through badly eroded land from desolate villages to spend scarce coins at the trading station. The way that wealth attracts reverse mercantilism is also illustrated by workers' long commutes to large, expensive cities from cheaper, more distant communities, as in Ontario. One picture illustrates extreme urban poverty.

In the South African native reserves there is not enough land to support the population agriculturally, and not enough other resources to develop industrially. The system of migrant labour that developed supported the reserves poorly and flooded the cities with unemployed workers. This serious double problem requires the four-tier resolution described in chapter 4 and below.

Figure 4. Unemployed Slum Dweller with Child, from "Uprooting Poverty, The South African Challenge", Francis Wilson and Mamphela Ramphele, Carnegie Report, W. W. Norton, 1989 (with permission)

Trinidad and Tobago were settled by European colonizers using slaves or indentured labourers. Then oil was found and the oil and gas industry transformed the economy, initially stimulating it, then rapidly growing until it overexpanded the export economy with substantial problems amid wealth. Wages rose so high, protected products became so expensive, and the currency remained so strong that unemployment rose as the unprotected industries closed down, inflation accelerated, and people began to worry about the future, some even fleeing the country. The paper attached as Appendix A (The "Dutch Disease" Problem), written at the request of the Consul General for Trinidad and Tobago in Toronto, shows how complex policy solutions could be. Further oil and gas discoveries have made Trinidad rich—too rich to bother with other industries and agriculture—and very inflationary, more like the oil sheikdoms of the Middle East than a diversified economy. When the oil and gas go, what then?

Another request for my advice came in respect of the Caribbean islands of Grenada and St. Kitts and the small economy of Zimbabwe, in Africa. Under the heading "Colonial Past and Poverty-Stricken Present," I argued that mercantilism plus imperialism plus colonialism plus capitalism led to the creation of empires, with plantations and slave labour in the colonies exporting raw materials to the motherland. After the slaves were freed, populations exploded and land reforms proceeded, but raw material prices remained low and the soil became eroded and exhausted. As a result, these previous colonies became unprofitable and impoverished and were largely abandoned by their colonizers. Mercantilism came to mean "exploit cheap labour and resources until they are played out, then abandon them and put up tariffs against their products." The former colonies responded with emigration of significant parts of the population, temporary labour migration to earn money to send back home, and "exporting" the services of the land, climate, and beaches or game reserves in the form of tourism. (Unfortunately, another form of the "Dutch disease" resulted, with profits and wages in the tourism sector becoming so high that other sectors could not compete for land or labour, and workers were no longer satisfied with previously low wages, so unemployment and the export of labour abroad increased.)

In other words, the small islands of the West Indies are also adopting reverse mercantilism for survival by migrating to the industrial centres or selling tourism services to the rich. Their populations now depend on personal access to the metropolitan centres and/or peoples. But since such access could be cut off,[1] another type of reverse mercantilism, involving goods—that is, exporting manufactured goods "duty free" to the metropoles—should be tried, in the form of free trade in selected commodities that have been judged not to harm the rich trading partners' economies.

There can thus be four types of reverse mercantilism: (1) migration and migrant labour, (2) personal access to sell services, (3) free trade in selected goods, and (4) "turn-around" mercantilism, as in Canada.

The first section of chapter 2 discusses the introduction of parallel, gold-backed commodity money as a savings vehicle alongside the existing unbacked bank money to protect savings against inflation, discourage inflationary behaviour, and thus reduce inflation. Policymakers would then not have to fear inflation so much when they consider employment-creating stimulative policies, nor have to introduce strict anti-inflation recession policies, thereby perpetuating or worsening unemployment and poverty. In these ways, parallel commodity money could indirectly reduce poverty.[2] Parallel commodity money also directly reduces poverty by creating non-inflationary money, additional real and exportable goods and jobs in their making, more purchasing power like exports, multiplier benefits, etc.

Chapter 2 then goes on to discuss how we became dependent on unbacked bank money in the first place, creating the need for a parallel backed currency to prevent eventual runaway inflation. Without this parallel backed currency, inflation continues and the inflationary bank-money system eventually leads to defensive anti-inflation policies that threaten to create unemployment and more poverty. As a result, we again need parallel commodity money. The present low inflation rate, as measured by a super-strong oil export-supported currency, cannot last (measured in US dollars, the Canadian inflation rate is rising quickly). The unbacked bank money can eventually become so inflationary (or worthless) that it threatens the world unbacked money system (as now) alternately with deflation. This monetary insecurity is potentially the greatest threat of poverty.

We might wonder why a government central bank could not lend the right, non-inflationary amount so as to stimulate both supply and demand and fight poverty without inflation. One reason is that a government with the power to create money would not be able to resist demands for funds from all sides. Therefore we would have to return to the system of private banks lending a somewhat restricted amount of money at restrictive interest rates, at risk and for profit, with a broad limit on the money supply being set by central bank "bank rates." But this mechanism does not completely stop inflation and recession. Banks charge bank-money interest on bank-money loans that have to be repaid in bank money. Therefore more bank money has to be created to pay that interest, so the money supply has to be expanded exponentially, which is essentially inflationary. Moreover, private bank money creation and lending cannot alleviate poverty for the following reasons:

- It finances only those who are creditworthy and reasonably rich and does not help the poor and un-creditworthy. It therefore increases the gap between rich and poor and the overall amount of poverty.
- It facilitates the process whereby good land, housing and other real estate, resources, and business opportunities

gravitate into the hands of the rich, contributing to a socioeconomic and environmental inequality catastrophe that worsens poverty and inadequate demand cumulatively, partly by creating unemployment.

- As mentioned above, it creates inflation, then restrictive anti-inflation policies that generate unemployment and poverty.

On the other hand, if government created and lent the unbacked money with no strict anti-inflation controls, hyperinflation and currency collapse could occur. We could conclude that money creation creates poverty and/or hyperinflation and dispossession, no matter what we do, unless we introduce a gold-backed parallel commodity money. But *lack* of money creation also creates depression and poverty. What on earth can we do? This artificially created money buys up the world's real estate and resources (as in Canada) and creates international inequality, poverty, and conflict, leading to world inflation, depression, poverty, and war. The result: at the least, billions (more) will become poverty-stricken. *Nothing other than reform of the bank debt-money system through parallel commodity money will tackle the poverty of nations.*

After the above theoretical analysis, it is a relief to be able to add Appendix B (A Parallel Currency System for South Africa), which contains a potential practical application. The problems of unbacked money are not solvable with an unbacked money system alone, but they are also not solvable with a backed monetary system alone. The first system leads eventually to exponentially accelerating inflation, while the second system, by not expanding rapidly enough, leads quickly to deflationary collapse. Therefore the two monetary systems must run together in parallel so as to promote greater economic expansion and security, reduce inflation and check instability, and save the economy from collapse.

Chapter 3 turns to discussing ideology (inequality) as it relates to diagnoses or causes of unequal income distribution, unemployment, and poverty, centring around the concept of inadequate demand. Marxist analysis says that under capitalism there is inadequate demand, causing depression, impoverishment of the proletariat, unemployment, and poverty, leading to war in the search for new markets and profits. Therefore, capitalism, or private ownership of the means of production, and the inadequate demand that results are the main causes of poverty, and these faults are to be remedied by revolution and expropriation, putting the means of production in the hands of the state.

Socialist doctrine holds that misery and injustice, unemployment and poverty, are the result of the division of society into rich and poor, which unequal division is to be remedied by tax redistribution and the welfare state. That is, inequality and inadequate demand, the basic causes of unemployment and poverty, are to be remedied by greater equality, but not specifically by expropriation.

Keynes agreed that unemployment and poverty are due to inadequate demand, and that the welfare state could be part of the solution. But he argued that the capitalist system was the best means of running the economy, and opposed confiscation of private property and heavy taxation. He felt poverty should be remedied by deficit spending and low interest rates to create employment and adequate demand.

Monetarism and New Right theories oppose all the above, especially Keynesian expansionism, and declare that expansionism, the welfare state, and money supply increases lead to inflation, high taxes, welfare dependency, and inadequate supply as the basic causes of poverty. Therefore one must cut taxes and government spending to reduce poverty.

The Environment and Human Ecology

Chapter 4 then rounds out the foursome of recommended policy measures—reverse mercantilism and parallel commodity money, plus review of ideologies—by discussing environmentally sound agricultural, rural, and regional development. The discussion starts by looking down at the earth from above. When we do this, we can see the complexity of the lands and seas from which different peoples extract their food and resources, often leaving deserts or dead seas behind them and very frequently living a life of poverty. The cities in turn are becoming terribly overcrowded and poverty-stricken on the fringes, partly because of the constant, massive rural-urban influx, and partly because of faults in the bank-money systems causing worsening unemployment. Ecological degradation, population explosion, inequality, migration, and monetary instability are threatening to become major world poverty problems along with pollution/global warming and soil erosion.

Economics and environmentalism should therefore work together, for otherwise there will be neither the jobs and money needed to get the environmental work done nor a liveable planet on which to enjoy the fruits of our labour. Not only is infinite development impossible in a finite world, but finite development of the wrong kind can also cause poverty, environmental destruction, human disaster. and potentially worse poverty to come. These very real problems exist already and combine to help produce the worsening socioeconomic, environmental, and political disasters, or "failed state" scenarios, that are springing up despite so-called development.

The marginalized people from less developed or destroyed/developed hinterlands transfer their poverty and social problems to, and intensify them in, polluted, heavily unemployed, socially devastated, and unequal cities at home and abroad, leading to socioeconomic and environmental crises in their new homes as well as in their old. The resulting crises threaten corporations, capital, and the elites who might otherwise employ the poor, engendering capital flight and elite emigration, which threaten to leave the poor not only to suffer and starve in abject poverty but also to live with no solution in sight and no hope beyond crime and even terrorism. This problem is so great that out-migration is likely to be a major future issue.

Final Thoughts

The set of poverty causes described in this book—namely mercantilistic rural decline feeding into rural-urban migration and urban overcrowding, unemployment, inequality, and poverty, requiring monetary and distributional reforms to stimulate urban prosperity and provide financing for rural recovery—does not cover all poverty situations, but it does cover enough of the world to warrant separate study, such as in this book. It is exciting to see the story developing, in all its tragedy and danger, and then devise suggested solutions to the causes. It is a thesis worth pursuing. The parallel commodity money hypothesis alone is a contribution to economic theory that is applicable everywhere, and probably necessary to prevent economic collapse. The reader and the public will be well rewarded.

Corrigendum

In the above text, I hardly mentioned population control. There were two main reasons for this: ideological opposition from people I respect; and concern about possible population reduction (!) due to environmental and natural disasters, warfare, disease and other causes. But, since omission might be misleading, as overpopulation can be a crisis in itself, let this book recognize this, but argue that *Tackling the Poverty of Nations* is not intended to reduce populations, even though reduced populations might reduce poverty, but to support populations and let them choose.

POSTSCRIPT

Without questioning the arguments in the book, I note that recent events have suggested highlighting the sections of the book dealing with potentials of monetary collapse and what could be done to prevent the latter (parallel commodity money), because the events described could be amongst the worst causes of world-wide poverty.

APPENDIX A

The "Dutch Disease" Problem

Excerpts from "A Critique of the 'Dutch Disease': Problem Analysis for Trinidad and Tobago with Recommended Solutions" (February 2007)[1]

General Analytical Setting and General Solutions

When a large export industry starts or grows in a town, region or country, it changes the whole character of its host location. It brings in outside money, employs and pays local labour, purchases local goods and services, pays taxes to the local government and expands the local economy. The outside money passes from the initial recipients (converted into local currency) to others, multiplying its effect and increasing its impact, until almost everyone and every organization is wholly or partially/indirectly dependent on it—until it declines or shuts down! Existing local trade-related industries, which exported or competed with imports, decline in importance relatively or even absolutely, as the economy expands and labour and other resources are bid away from them at higher prices. Meanwhile, non-trade-dependent activities, relying on the expansion of the local economy brought about by the export earnings, tend to expand—and the domestic economy becomes characterized by activities catering to the local population: "taking in each other's washing." Almost the whole local economy becomes dependent on the new or expanding export industry, and if that industry is a resource industry, on the life of that resource. The economy becomes vulnerable to resource and outside forces.

In Trinidad and Tobago, when the large oil and gas industry boomed, it injected huge foreign exchange money supply increases into the domestic economy, raised wage levels, increased demands and prices for local goods and services, and ballooned central Government revenues and expenditures. All these expansions would have been inflationary in themselves. But the inflationary impacts were worsened by the facts that the injections were of foreign currency and that energy sector wages were much higher than pre-existing average T&T wages.

In the case of the large foreign exchange injections, there was, first of all, the foreign exchange "multiplier"—the dollars were spent again and again before they "leaked" abroad; then there was the foreign exchange strengthening—the economy could expand further than in the case of an injection of domestic currency spending, because foreign exchange constraints would not so quickly force a slowdown; thirdly, the T&T dollar was strengthened (or held steady by Central Bank interventions, e.g., through expanding the local money supply, income and imports), despite inflation, so that local trade-related industries were not protected from inflation by devaluation, and began to shrink or fail—meaning less product facing more demand, creating even more inflation, and the appearance of "de-industrialization," which killed productive jobs and made the country even more dependent on the energy resource export sector for foreign exchange. (The alternative of devaluation would have meant yet more inflation—a double bind.)

In the case of high energy sector wages, wages in the non-energy sectors were bid upwards, raising supply costs (inflation again) and reducing trade-related industry competitiveness. This effect was aggravated by militant trade unions demanding higher wages, monopolistic businesses raising mark-ups, and massive government spending increases, increasing demand [in addition to] supply cost increases, and contributing to the current 10% p.a. inflation rate, which has everyone worried—and rightly so, because inflation contributes to inflation.

Meanwhile, data illustrate the extreme dependence of the economy on the energy export sector (which will eventually decline). This sector contributes 41% of GDP, mostly in foreign exchange, and even more if the export multiplier (the domestic spending of this revenue) is taken into account. The non-energy trade-related industries contribute only about 7% of GDP. The resulting competitive near 50% of GDP supports government and other non-competitive non-trade-related activities, constituting over 50% of first-round GDP spending, and almost all if derivative rounds of domestic spending are included. These data illustrate that T&T has an almost totally oil-and-gas dependent economy, comparable to the oil economics of the Middle East, despite more favourable land, water and climate resources. There is very little self-sufficiency provided by the non-trade-related bulk of the population and labour forces for a population accustomed to imported basics and luxuries to fall back on in case of energy sector decline. Therefore, greater self-sufficiency and new export industries are absolutely essential for the long-run survival of the T&T economy, population, labour force and livelihood/subsistence, and for avoidance of collapse.

The above requires us to think hard and clearly, to find ways out of this dependence-plus-inflation predicament. Let us make a start as follows (in general terms, with more detail below).

General

Practical specifics are necessary, and some are outlined below, but we must also be guided by a clear picture of our general goals and needs. To tackle the predicament in which T&T has become almost totally dependent on the energy export sector, which is directly and indirectly contributing to accelerating inflation, we need export promotion (from the non-energy sectors), import substitution and as much in anti-inflation measures as possible. Put another way, the general need is for improved export competitiveness and greater competitive self-sufficiency. How? Through productive investment (of energy and government revenues), plus subsidized investment of industrial and population savings, plus direct and indirect industrial and agricultural subsidies (subsidized wages are better than subsidized welfare, and are less inflationary because output is increased). The most general subsidy is devaluation, but since this is highly inflationary, it should be a last resort, and prices should be held down by investing rather than consumption spending of energy revenues, by freer trade (lower tariffs), savings incentives, and a parallel gold-backed currency system.

Specific

Specific measures could include cost-reducing government capital investments (including investments in human capital); cost-reducing operating subsidies (such as the above subsidized wages); subsidies and private and government investments in specific trade-related projects, such as "tropical paradise" settlements, bringing in foreign exchange, and agricultural and rural development projects. They could also include fiscal reforms, such as lower deficits, more steeply progressive income taxes and lower sales taxes and import duties to spread the wealth and fight inflation. Monetarily, or strategically, they could further include slowing down oil and gas extraction, to prolong energy life and reduce inflation, investing some revenues in a parallel gold-backed currency system to reduce inflation and thus fight it, and attracting foreign investment only into trade-related industries to help promote and share in the more efficient T&T economy.

Let us now add some local input, with some notes from the T&T Chamber of Industry and Commerce magazine, *Contact*,[2] dealing with "Dutch Disease," then add some specific detail on (a) Parallel Commodity Money; (b) Export Promotion and Import Substitution; and (c) Agricultural and Rural Development. Chamber findings were:

- What is typical for resource-based economies is a decline in the trade-related industries of manufacturing and agriculture (due to world competition for rising-cost firms), contrasted with expansion in non-trade-related sectors such as government, construction, transport, retail, professional and other services, which depend on the domestic spending of large and growing resource revenues, and are not price sensitive.
- Natural resource (export) growth leads to the de-industrialization and reduced diversification of the dependent economy.

- Too much resource (export converted to domestic) money chasing too few (domestic) goods produces inflation; while too much foreign exchange earnings leads to a strong dollar, closures of uncompetitive industries, unemployment and poverty (partially offset by expanded non-trade-related industry and government spending).

- "Dutch Disease" refers to the harmful consequences of large increases in a country's foreign income.

- The booming oil and gas or energy sector is able to pay higher wages than the rest of the competitive or trade-related economy. This Dutch Disease forces the average wage rate up, causing labour-intensive trade-related industries to decline; but the state, in receipt of large tax and foreign exchange revenues of the energy sector, engages in an expansion of spending, creating virtually full employment and increased inflation—a "slippery slope" from which it is difficult to recover. Inflation, in turn, makes the exchange rate seem overvalued, favouring imports (and capital flight) and depressing local trade-related industry further.

- These problems lead to calls for devaluation (which would mean yet more inflation and capital flight), which is resisted by the Central Bank. The island economy comes to resemble a one-industry town. The only activities growing rapidly are non-tradable services (including government) spending strong oil revenues. But the government, awash with revenues and jobs, does not believe T&T suffers from Dutch Disease, and the University of the West Indies prefers the term "Open Petroleum Economy," dependence on which makes T&T very vulnerable.

- Natural resource booms also bring adverse side effects: There were clear signs of overheating due to Dutch Disease; the wages and numbers of labourers and construction workers increased suddenly; fiscal indiscipline led to yielding to calls by militant trade unions for an increasing share of the oil rents; government wages rose enormously, over 13 times, as did government spending on transfers and subsidies.

- The economy of T&T continues to grow strongly, up 12% in 2006, driven by increased activity in the energy sector, up 20.65% in 2006, and accounting for 41.2% of total GDP. The exchange rage has been stable. But inflation is now the main challenge (assuming non-consideration of future energy decline). Inflation has accelerated, real estate prices are rising, industry is keeping its cash balances offshore, capacity constraints are evident in some sectors, and the labour market has tightened. Labour is being paid higher wages, but there isn't an accompanying increase in productivity, so costs and prices are rising. Government spending is more on social infrastructure than on directly productive activities.

These descriptive comments are very clear and revealing, but they do not proffer any solutions.

Specific Analyses

Possible Help from Parallel Commodity Money

In the above text, it was indicated that inflation and uncompetitive trade-related domestic industry were major problems in T&T. It was noted that even devaluation (and more inflation) may have to be considered at some time in the future. In such an economic and monetary atmosphere, people, to protect themselves and their savings, tend to think about inflation-hedge assets and capital flight, both of which accelerate inflation in a vicious circle. As indicated above, inflation is a "slippery slope," which is very difficult to recover from. But the proposal of a gold-backed parallel currency, into which people could safely invest their savings, is a way around this problem. It says: let the banking system manage the bank-money system, to preserve prosperity and reasonable stability, with the exception of some inflation; but establish a parallel, gold-backed monetary system, into which people could put their savings to protect them from inflation, with the units of the two monetary systems being "convertible," or exchangeable into each other at market-determined prices . . . .

In uncertain-currency nations there sometimes is a national currency and the US dollar operating in parallel, with people favouring the US dollar for savings, travel abroad, capital flight, buying assets sold only for US dollars, etc., but otherwise mainly using the local currency for everything else. This is a sort of dual/parallel monetary system, which could be left in place, but it would miss other important features of the gold-backed parallel currency system, such as better protection against inflation (the US dollar has recently been in decline) and the benefits of this labour-plus-government-mint-created currency going to the government and the people, not to the banks (the coins would not be "debt-money").

APPENDIX B

A Parallel Currency System for South Africa

I n 1998 I wrote to South Africa's Department of Finance about the idea of a gold-backed parallel currency system. Maria Ramos, the department's director general, replied:

> Following the success of the Krugerrand, a private sector initiative, the Chamber of Mines negotiated the right to be able to sell up to one third of South Africa's gold production in approved value added forms each with a mass of 1 kg or less. The balance of production had to be sold to the South African Reserve Bank in terms of Exchange Control Regulations. As you may be aware, from 12 December 1997, gold producers have been able to apply for exemption from the relevant Exchange Control Regulations to enable them to sell all their gold production directly to counterparties of their choice,

and not to the Reserve Bank, as has up to now been the case. This step represents the latest move in the phased withdrawal of the Reserve Bank/Department of Finance from purchases and sales of gold.

I am, therefore, pleased that you have sent your proposal to the Chamber of Mines enclosing details about the scheme offered by the Royal Canadian mint. It is possible that the gold producers, the Rand Refinery of the South African Mint may elect to produce a "four-nines" 1 oz gold coin with or without buy-back guarantees, but then that will be a commercial decision by the private sector. The possible success of such a venture would flow through to the gold producers and this could enhance employment creation. The private sector, however, must do the feasibility study to assess the potential risks and rewards.

In 2000, inspired by an article about him in *The Economist*, I wrote to Dr. T. T. Mboweni, governor of the South African Reserve Bank:

Bank money is created out of nothing, and has its value determined by supply and demand—or convertibility or exportability to the United States—as influenced by interest rates. The determination of value by convertibility no longer applies in terms of a scarce precious metal like gold, but only to convertibility in terms of what money will buy and what the sellers can get for it, and so on ad infinitum—a circle broken by inflation. However, since private banks have the power and the will to create ever more money at interest, there is a constant tendency for the bank money supply to expand exponentially toward worthlessness. This puts the controlling central bank in the unenviable position of either having to squash inflation with high interest rates and create worse unemployment, or having to allow inflation to continue wreaking havoc and destroy savings. The "Goldilocks" situation of growth without inflation is a matter of good fortune which cannot last, especially when a nation is plagued with high unemployment.

My solution is as follows: Mine and mint a parallel currency to protect savings—e.g., a "Mandela Rand" of 1 oz. gold, differing from the Krugerrand in that it would have a face value somewhat above its gold value and would be redeemable at that face value—so that people could protect their savings (or gold miners could buy land), while the transactions economy worked with bank money. Under such an arrangement, the central bank could create more jobs in two ways: first by employing more gold miners, and second by eventually not having to crush inflation so severely. Furthermore, the draining effect of capital flight could be lessened by producing more exportable gold, in such a form that those who want to take their money out can take it in the form of an exported manufactured artifact (labour value) of gold, without depressing either the economy or the rand (because their purchasing power will go to the domestic producers of the gold). Exports would be increased, the rand supported, inflation combatted and maybe even the money supply could be increased to fight unemployment: just what South Africa needs.

With this letter, I enclosed a copy of my *Alternative Economics* paper "Alternative Monetary Theory, Practice, and Resolution."

The reply from the governor's office stated: "The Governor found your thoughts very interesting and commented that the idea of the Mandela Rand is receiving attention locally and may perhaps materialise some time in the future. Acting [on] his recommendation, your paper on *Alternative Monetary Theory, Practice, and Resolution* has been distributed amongst the economists in the Bank's Research Department."

APPENDIX C

Agricultural Production Subsidies in Malawi

An article by Stephanie Nolen in the *Globe and Mail*[1] describes one of the most productive ways to tackle rural poverty: by subsidizing rural industry. "Over the past couple of years, Malawi has broken with an orthodoxy long advocated by Canada and other Western donor nations: The impoverished country has gone back to subsidizing poor farmers." She goes on to add, "the subsidies have been a raging success." Patrick Kabambe of the Ministry of Agriculture and Food Security is quoted describing why his country made this move: "People are so poor they use recycled seed and no fertilizer. They can't meet their needs that way and they grow no surplus. People sink deeper and deeper into poverty. It's a vicious cycle. We had to do something."

Farmers are given coupons to allow them to purchase fertilizer and seed at deeply discounted prices. The result has been an increase in the average yield from 800 kg per hectare to 2 tonnes.

The subsidies have produced a "record harvest, a massive surplus of the staple crop . . . particularly gratifying in Malawi, a country that has been plagued with critical food shortages several times in the past decade." The program was expensive, but less so than the cost of imported food aid after years of donor-advised scrapping of subsidies in favour of "free markets."

It should be noted that the agricultural economics literature is full of concerns about instability and low prices that could not be dealt with through the above subsidies. Farmers can be devastated by crashing prices for record crops, by poor weather conditions of many kinds, by diseases and pests, soil erosion and drought, poor storage facilities, lack of transport, and so on. Input subsidies cover only low yields. This is not to downplay the above success, nor to miss the importance of subsidizing production rather than non-work, but only to warn those involved to be prepared for other disasters.

NOTES

Introduction

[1] Adam Smith, *The Wealth of Nations* (Chicago: University of Chicago Press, 1976), 450.

[2] Francis Wilson and Mamphela Ramphele, *Uprooting Poverty: The South African Challenge. A Report for the Second Carnegie Inquiry into Poverty and Development in Southern Africa* (New York: W. W. Norton, 1989).

[3] *The Life and Times of Daniel Lindley* (London: Epworth Press, 1949), 247. Lindley was a missionary to the Zulus, pastor of the Voortrekkers, and a founder of the Dutch Reformed Church.

[4] The money income of such regions or nations (say, $Y per year) consists of export dollars still present being spent locally

before they leak outside the jurisdiction, that is, export dollars multiplied by the number of times each is spent locally on average before they leak away ($E per year). Thus regional money income is equal to $Y = $E × C, where C is the average number of times each dollar circulates or is spent on local goods and services within the region before leaking away abroad.

[5] This can be expressed by the formula $Y = (E \times \frac{1}{2}) + (E \times \frac{1}{2} \times \frac{1}{2}) + (E \times \frac{1}{2} \times \frac{1}{2} \times \frac{1}{2}) \ldots = E \times (\frac{1}{2} + \frac{1}{4} + \frac{1}{8} \ldots) = E \times 1$.

Chapter 1: Tackling Poverty Through Trade and Migration

[1] Today we speak of the four functions of money as a means of trade or instrument of commerce, a measure of value, a store of value, and a unit of account. John Kenneth Galbraith said: "Some have always wanted money for what it would buy. Some have wanted it for the power it conferred. Some have sought it for the prestige it provided. The Scotch wanted it for its own sake" (*The Scotch*, Penguin Books, 1966). Money also provides security, although that function is now partly replaced by welfare, medicare, and pensions. If bank debt money lost value, we would be in trouble unless a stable commodity money system was already in place.

2 Adam Smith, *The Wealth of Nations* (Chicago: University of Chicago Press, 1976), 450.

3 Ibid., 452, 455.

4 Ibid., 472-73.

5 Cambridge, MA: Harvard University Press, 1960.

6 Cf. Mel Watkins' staple theory, discussed later.

7 Canada imports raw sugar free but imposes very high duties on refined sugar, thus forcing poor countries to export cheap raw sugar while Canada benefits from the sugar-refining industry, with product prices many times higher than those for imported raw sugar and with jobs that are less demanding and higher paid.

8 The United States, recognizing this, won't sell U.S. oil resources or gold to China for U.S. dollars. And Canada won't give back Aboriginal lands stolen by treaty. I am living on former Native land that I was able to buy with hard-earned "money" but which I won't sell except for many times more money (because of inflation and also its

real developed value). Natives can't earn that much money because of discrimination against them. So Natives are poor and dispossessed because of theft sanctioned by law and enforced by property rights, plus money values, inflation, and discrimination—right here, by us. Mercantile history, conquest, expropriation or theft, racism, and discrimination are major reasons for poverty.

9   The "staple theory" maintained that "the pace of development in Canada is determined fundamentally by the exports that enable Canada to pay its way in the world." See Melville H. Watkins, "A Staple Theory of Economic Growth," *Canadian Journal of Economics and Political Science* 24:2 (May 1963), 142. The theory argued that "staple exports are the leading sector of the economy and set the pace for economic growth . . . . Economic development will be a process of diversification around an export base" (144). There are some interesting parallels between mercantilism and the staple theory.

10 *Globe and Mail* (May 21, 2007), B2, quoting Statistics Canada data.

11 Now that Canadian gold and oil are shooting up to multiyear or record highs and the U.S. dollar and interest rates are tumbling to record or multiyear lows (as of May 2008), we can expect the liquidity-increasing, recession-threatened U.S. economy to

pump up its money supplies so much that rapid inflation will reappear just down the road, leading to inflationary recession and a reversal of monetary policy back to high interest rates. This policy ambivalence is likely to spread through the markets, creating uncertainty everywhere, especially regarding the value of money and security of income, leading to a future that is hard to predict. Money may possibly become hyperinflationary but/or hard to get hold of, the values of assets could soar or go bust, and the value of jobs could disappear overnight. What has all this got to do with poverty? A very great deal: many millions of people could lose their jobs and/or the value of their savings, and the government and the banks will be unable to do anything about it because they will have blown their credibility, having fooled the people with worthless money that they believed in, worked for, saved, and invested. The parallel commodity money recommended in this book is therefore an invaluable insurance against collapse. All other investments are at risk.

[12] This list comes from a term paper I prepared at the University of Toronto in 1966.

[13] We could, without harm, help poor countries to produce what we need but do not produce, by means of low or zero tariffs on selected products from them and even production assistance with capital goods, skilled personnel, and so on, to really help

people help themselves. An example might be winter fruits and vegetables being governed by tariffs only in the summer.

14   Marilyn Bidgood, of the Elmvale office of the provincial Ministry of Agriculture and Food, has calculated that, in 1986, net agricultural incomes in North Simcoe averaged only $5,925 per farm (probably with two or more workers each), compared with average male full-time earnings in Simcoe County of $27,400 per person.

15   This, my fourth, book is about the poverty I have seen around me, about the apparent causes of and possible remedies for that poverty, and about searching for the fundamental theories that explain such poverty and what needs to be done to remove it. In this task, I started with Adam Smith's fundamental mathematical/logical and mercantilist principles for promoting the wealth of nations, namely that "the great affair, we always find, is to get money," and that "money is obtained by a favourable balance of trade" (nowadays, by bank-money creation). Derived from these principles, any economic unit must seek to promote exports to bring money in and to substitute for imports to keep money circulating domestically, in order to promote the wealth—that is, tackle the poverty—of nations.

Mathematically, in a region without the ability to create its own ("convertible") money, exports or money coming in from outside constitute the money supply until they leak abroad in imports. The region's income ($Y p.a.) consists of the spending of these export dollars ($E p.a.) locally. In other words, income $Y = $E, multiplied by the number of times each dollar circulates locally before leaking away; this latter is represented by 1/m, where m is the average fraction of spending leaking abroad in each round of spending: $Y = $E/m. For example, if m = ½ and E = 1, then Y will equal 2. But exports ($E p.a.) must be greater than or equal to imports ($M p.a.); otherwise there would be less and less money left for spending on imports or domestic products. Or, if artificial money (e) was being created in the nation such that imports (M) exceeded exports (E), the value of that money being created out of nothing would be decreasing. Therefore, mY must be less than or equal to E, or E sets an upper limit to Y (which it creates). If expansionary monetary and fiscal policies try to make Y greater than this limit, the currency will decline in value and the inflationary treadmill will begin. (Exports must remain greater than or equal to imports—$E \geq M = mY$ and $Y \leq E/m$—for money to retain its value.)

This leads to two conclusions: (1) If money (e) is unbacked confidence money, and monetary and fiscal policies are too expansionary (Y and/or M grow too fast), money will decline in value towards nothing. The only way to grow without inflation will be the mercantilist way of expanding exports (E) faster than imports (M), or achieving a "favourable balance of trade." But, since "confidence money" expands exponentially, Y and/or M will tend to grow too fast and confidence money will eventually self-destruct. Therefore, (2) the only way to avoid hyperinflationary collapse in the long run is to introduce a stable-value, real parallel commodity money alongside the declining-value unbacked bank money needed for trade and commerce. We thus seem to have discovered a fundamental truth about money in our search for ways to prevent (mass) poverty!

Following the above mathematical summary, this book outlines the major groups of poverty problems and remedies as follows:

1. tackling poverty through *trade and migration*: mercantilism and reverse mercantilism, based on the mercantilist principle that prosperity was brought about by a favourable balance of trade, which was the way of increasing money supplies before the banks created artificial bank money.

2. tackling poverty through *monetary reform*: remedying the inability of unbacked bank money systems to expand money supplies and relieve poverty and increase employment without inflation, by introducing a parallel, gold-backed commodity

money as a savings vehicle alongside unbacked bank
money.

3. tackling poverty through *demand and distribution reforms*: reviewing the great theorists to see what they had to say about income and wealth distribution, adequate and inadequate demand, unemployment and poverty, and their remedies through distribution reform (overlapping with supply-side land reform).

4. tackling poverty through *agricultural, rural, and regional development*: to remedy the poverty-led rural-urban influx to overcrowded, underemployed and poverty-stricken cities, through agricultural supply-side development, land-reform agricultural station establishments, and planned balanced development all round.

[16] $87/15 \div 13/75 = 87/15 \times 75/13 = 33.46$

[17] A friend asked me why I abandoned the survey, and I replied in all truth that it was because the land was a chaotic slum and I did not know where to go, what to do, or what to record, except that it was a "dormitory slum" of Durban. I could go on at length about switching to social science and trying to find alternatives to the urban whites' left-wing philosophies

that offered no solutions. I proposed more land for the
Africans, but no whites would give up land in South Africa.
This view persisted after de Klerk handed over power, but
not land, to Mandela, which has helped keep Africans poor
to this day. Once again international investments are going in
and improving white lands, while the black moonscapes are
continuing to deteriorate, confirming the view (reinforced by
Zimbabwe) that "you can't give land to blacks." I eventually
went to Oxford to study economic development, then ended
up in Canada and began the research that culminated in this
book.

18 Alan Paton, *Cry, the Beloved Country* (London: Jonathan Cape,
    1948), 1-2.

19 D. Hobart Houghton and Edith M. Walton, *The Economy of a
    Native Reserve* (Pietermaritzburg: Shuter and Shooter, 1952).

20 Ibid., 2.

21 Ibid., 3.

22 My parents, as missionaries, gave almost all their wealth away
    for religious reasons.

23 There was already an import duty of 25 percent on fully manufactured cars, so the proponents of this scheme claimed that prices would go down because of the cheap parts—which they never did.

24 $25/3 \times 100\% = 833\%$

25 A complete theoretical picture of an island with one profitable export industry could be constructed to show the problem(s) faced and what might be done about them. Appendix A shows the complicated path actually taken. It is worth noting that I have experienced mercantilistic cocoa estates, imperialistic oil discoveries, superior missionary stations, attempts to find export promotion and import substitution remedies, economic refugees caused by oil, criticism for being too mercantilistic (resulting in a failed PhD), and other attempts to help, all of which culminated in this book.

26 George Grant, "Creating Value Out of Nothing," *Alternative Economics* Occasional Paper no. 62 (25 October 2003), ISSN 1704-3522.

27 Ruth Glass, "The Inescapable Urge to Escape from the 'Carefree' Islands," *Globe and Mail*, 24 November 1961, 53A.

Chapter 2: Monetary Theory Reform

[1]　Note that parallel commodity monies have been successfully used both in individual countries and on the world scene. See this book's Foreword by Dr. Cliff Jutlah.

[2]　Now "reserves" tend to be ignored and monetary policy merely seeks to keep the consumer price index (CPI) inflation down to 2 percent. A letter from federal Minister of Finance James M. Flaherty (July 3, 2007) states: "The Bank of Canada abandoned the idea of targeting money growth in the early 1980s" and agreed with the government that "the Bank should conduct monetary policy aimed at keeping total CPI inflation at 2 percent"—excluding food, energy, and housing, the main components of the CPI. Money growth is inflation, so the approach is to keep money growth down with this false CPI measure and to forget unemployment and poverty, exchange rates, and other such realities.

[3]　Incidentally, it is very difficult to get bank gold in exchange for bank money, as you can find out by trying. What the banks do is to trade "commercial" gold at varying market prices (bought and sold in the market)—plus or minus mark-ups, commissions, handling charges, sales taxes, exchange rate conversions, etc.—to make you think that, because you can buy gold with money, gold stands behind money, even if not at a fixed rate. In this latter sense, everything stands behind

bank money except things that are not sold for money, such as land in some countries, and except when there is rapid inflation. Hence the banks' fear of inflation, which could make bank money worthless—until the next round, when they create enough money (out of nothing) to buy everything back again!

4   Today U.S. gold reserves are frozen. Foreigners, including the Chinese with all their U.S. dollars, cannot get U.S. gold anyway.

5   Then the "peasants" are unable get back their land and resources by any means: the money they create is not accepted, land treaties are not honoured, and they can't get gold for U.S. dollars.

6   It is very hard to break into and remain an accepted member of this close-knit club unless one is invited in for political reasons.

7   In fact, with the U.S. dollar presently (in early 2008) losing trustworthiness, *all* created bank money is under suspicion.

8   If convertible monies are convertible and other monies are not, then the world is immediately divided into money-haves and money-have-nots (the poor). Note that even convertible monies

are backed by nothing, so establishing a "world currency" would be no solution.

Chapter 3: Demand and Distribution Theories

1   An illustrative list is as follows: people with skills, motivation, education, tools and capital; entrepreneurs to bring productive resources together; workers to produce and consume; firms and corporations to organize production and sales; governments to make the rules and keep society together; land, energy, water, minerals, productive sales, and good climate; other resources, systems, and money that encourage productive motivation and effort; infrastructure, energy, peace, markets, ideologies, etc.

2   One solution to the danger of great inequality leading otherwise to communism is land reform of various types, plus cooperatives and milder forms of socialism.

3   Socialism's rules are simple: you take from the rich to give to the poor, and thereby alleviate poverty—for a time—by breaking the rules of the capitalist game, in which you got the reward you produced/earned and maybe didn't play if the rules were altered.

4   Note the similarity to mercantilist goals (trade surpluses spent at home) and Marxism and socialism (adequate demand or spending).

5 Keynes, like the mercantilists, Marxists, and socialists before him, sought a way of remedying poverty by increasing demand so that there was enough purchasing power to keep people employed. When Keynes's/bankers'/mercantilists' methods of increasing money supplies eventually led to inflation, the option chosen was basically restrictions on money supplies and government spending. The option favoured in this book—namely anti-inflationary parallel commodity money—has not been formally tried, and its case has to be made below. See also Clifford Jutlah's Foreword.

Chapter 4: Agricultural, Rural, and Regional Development

1 I was moved to pen the following little ditty, which may help readers remember this point (it can be sung to the tune of "Sarie Marais"):

> *Oh, get the money cir-cul-ating again,*
> *By bringing it to where there is none;*
> *And sending locals out to earn some more,*
> *And making bullion cash to keep the money sound.*
> *Then planning to invest in the places that are best,*
> *So that everywhere you go there is dough,*
> *And no one suffers poverty no more, no more,*
> *In this land that we all call home.*

2   To help make this program reach further, plot holders could graduate to become independent farmers or even managers of stations.

3   For example, the student-farmers might work under a foreman and receive a small wage and a share of the net profits.

4   George Grant, *Canadian Rural Development Lessons* (self-published, 1992), 3.

5   George Grant, "Creating Extra Values."

Chapter 5: Findings and Conclusions

1   See Glass, "The Inescapable Urge."

2   Starting now (as of May 2008), with gold around C$940 per ounce, coins could be struck with a face value of $100 and gold content of 0.05 ounce (worth C$48). Then the coins could be sold for a profit as a safety investment against both deflation and inflation—they would likely be snapped up. (If the value of gold decreases, the coins will retain their guaranteed face values—investors and pensioners can't lose).

Appendix A: The "Dutch Disease" Problem

1   Original sent via e-mail to Michael Lashley, Consul General for Trinidad and Tobago, Toronto, 29 February 2007. This version has been edited for length.

2   "The Economy: Dutch Disease," *Contact* 6:4 (2006).

Appendix C: Agricultural Production Subsidies in Malawi

1   Stephanie Nolen, "How Malawi went from a nation of famine to a nation of feast," *Globe and Mail*, 12 October 2007, A1.

BIBLIOGRAPHY

Brown, Lester R. *Plan B 2.0: Rescuing a Planet under Stress*. New York: W.W. Norton, 2006.

Carter, Vernon Gill, and Tom Dale. *Topsoil and Civilization*. Norman: University of Oklahoma Press, 1974.

Diamond, Jared. *Collapse: How Societies Choose to Fail or Succeed*. New York: Penguin, 2005.

Easterbrook, W. T., and Hugh G. J. Aitken. *Canadian Economic History*. Toronto: Macmillan, 1956.

Galbraith, J. K. *Money: Whence It Came, Where It Went*. Boston: Houghton Mifflin, 1975.

Glass, Ruth. "The Inescapable Urge to Escape from the 'Carefree' Islands." *Globe and Mail*, 24 November 1961, 53A

Grant, George R. *"Canada Savings Coins" or Commodity Money Parallel to Bank Money: A Proposal to Help Remove the Monetary (Demand) Causes of the Poverty of Nations*. Elmvale, ON: Team Publications, 1996.

——. *Canadian Rural Development Lessons*. Self-published, 1992.

——. *The Economic Analyst* (ISSN 0225-0845), 1997-2002.

—. *Trying to Help: Small Farms and Large Economies*. Self-published, 2005.

Griffin, Scott. *My Heart Is Africa: A Flying Adventure*. Toronto: Thomas Allen, 2006.

Houghton, D. Hobart, and Edith M. Walton. *The Economy of a Native Reserve: Keiskammahoek Rural Survey*. Vol. 2. Pietermaritzburg: Shuter and Shooter, 1952.

Jacks, G. V., and R. O. Whyte. *The Rape of the Earth*. London: Faber and Faber, 1939.

Keynes, J. M. *The General Theory of Employment, Interest and Money*. London: Macmillan, 1936.

Landes, David S. *The Wealth and Poverty of Nations*. New York: W.W. Norton, 1998.

Levin, Jonathan V. *The Export Economies*. Cambridge, MA: Harvard University Press, 1960.

Mackenzie, Norman. *Socialism: A Short History*. London: Hutchinson's Universal Library, 1949.

Myint, H. *The Economics of the Developing Countries*. London: Hutchinson's Universal Library, 1964.

Myrdal, Gunnar. *Economic Theory and Under-Developed Regions*. London: Duckworth, 1957.

Paton, Alan. *Cry, the Beloved Country*. London: Jonathan Cape, 1948.

Putnam, Donald F. *Canadian Regions*. Toronto: J. M. Dent & Sons, 1952.

Rifkin, Jeremy, and Ted Howard. *Entropy: Into the Greenhouse World*. New York: Bantam, 1981.

Samuelson, Paul A., & Anthony Scott. *Economics*. 2nd Canadian ed. Toronto: McGraw-Hill, 1968.

Smith, Adam. *The Wealth of Nations*. 1776. Reprint: University of Chicago Press, 1976.

Smith, Edwin W. *The Life and Times of Daniel Lindley*. London: Epworth Press, 1940.

Strathern, Paul. *Dr. Strangelove's Game: A Brief History of Economic Genius*. Toronto: Knopf, 2001.

Trinidad and Tobago Chamber of Industry and Commerce. "The 'Dutch Disease.'" *Contact* 6:4 (October 2006).

Watkins, Melville H. "A Staple Theory of Economic Growth." *Canadian Journal of Economics and Political Science* 29:2 (May 1963).

Watkins, M. H., and D. F. Forster. *Economics: Canada*. Toronto: McGraw-Hill, 1963.

Wilson, Francis, and Mamphela Ramphele. *Uprooting Poverty: The South African Challenge* (Carnegie Commission Report). New York: W. W. Norton, 1989.